THE WAY
WE WERE

Even students who don't know there has been a controversy "get the point" by reading Fisher's fine book. It is amazing how much and how well he pulls things together in his usual accessible style. I plan to use the book in a class for laypersons on Baptist history and distinctives. I don't know of a better book for that purpose.

—Sheri Adams
Gardner-Webb University
Boiling Springs, NC

The Way We Were is a sensitive, exquisitely written treatment of the way Southern Baptist life was and what it has become since the "recent unpleasantness," during which a new leadership has arisen in the denomination and conservatives and moderates have been at war with each other. Surely no writer has so successfully attempted to describe the history, theology, ecclesiology, and hymnody of Southern Baptists in terms designed to heal the present rift and draw the belligerent factions together again.

—John Killinger
Samford University
Birmingham, AL

The Way We Were is a must read for every Baptist. In this easy-to-read doctrinal history, Fisher Humphreys follows the threads that have been woven together to form the fabric of 21st century Southern Baptists. Without delving into the politics and the personalities that have so often defined Baptists, Humphreys takes the high road and allows the reader to look at the ideas and theological concepts that have distinguished and that have divided Southern Baptists. A careful reading my cause you to wonder if present-day Southern Baptists may have abandoned the way called straight and narrow to embark on a path that is only narrow.

—*Gary D. Fenton*
Pastor, Dawson Baptist Church
Birmingham, AL

With an irenic spirit and refreshing honesty, Fisher Humphreys explores history, theology, hymns and the Bible to understand the Southern Baptist controversy. He asks the central question about the conflict that dismembered the nation's largest Protestant denomination: Are Baptists better off now than in 1979? His book deserves study in churches brave enough to ask the question.

—*Robert M. Parham*
Executive Director of the
Baptist Center for Ethics

Smyth & Helwys Publishing, Inc.
6316 Peake Road
Macon, Georgia 31210-3960
1-800-747-3016
© 2002 by Smyth & Helwys Publishing

2nd Printing

Printed in the United States of America.

The paper used in this publication meets the minimum requirements of American National
Standard for Information Sciences—Permanence
of Paper for Printed Library Materials.
ANSI Z39.48–1984. (alk. paper)

Library of Congress Cataloging-in-Publication Data

Humphreys, Fisher.
 The way we were / by Fisher Humphreys.
  p. cm.
 Includes bibliographical references.
 ISBN 1-57312-376-5 (pbk)
 1. Southern Baptist Convention—Doctrines.
 2. Baptists—Doctrines.
 3. Church controversies—Baptists—History—20th century.
 I. Title

 BX6462.7 .H86 2002
 230'.6132—dc21

            2001055123
             CIP

THE WAY WE WERE

HOW SOUTHERN BAPTIST THEOLOGY HAS CHANGED AND WHAT IT MEANS TO US ALL

FISHER HUMPHREYS

REVISED EDITION

SMYTH&HELWYS
PUBLISHING, INCORPORATED • MACON, GEORGIA

TO DR. S. B. PLATT
AND TO THE MEMORY OF MRS. CLARA PLATT,
AND TO THE FIRST BAPTIST CHURCH
OF COLUMBUS, MISSISSIPPI,
WHO FIRST TAUGHT ME THE THEOLOGY
OF THE SOUTHERN BAPTISTS

CONTENTS

FOREWORD

Let me begin with the author. In Fisher Humphreys you are reading one of the very best Baptist theological minds at work today. His is a theological mind informed by shrewd historical awareness and tempered by a devout and magnanimous Christian spirit. And as if that were not enough, Fisher Humphreys claims one of the deftest literary hands, marked by utter clarity, to be found in Baptist academic circles.

All of this is to say that Humphreys thinks theologically, historically, Christianly, and baptistically. And what he thinks, he communicates on the written page with disarming simplicity and uncanny precision. Humphreys writes theology the way Fred Craddock preaches the gospel. Scholarship is never paraded or worn on the sleeve, but you can never doubt that the theological pail is being drawn from an exceptionally deep intellectual well. Few people with a Southern Baptist background could write so dispassionately or knowledgeably about such an incendiary Baptist conflict as has Fisher Humphreys.

What about the book itself? It is a book about the theological dimensions of the controversy that shook the foundations of the Southern Baptist Convention during the decades of the 80s and 90s. That controversy began at the national level, far from most Baptist laypeople, trickled down to the state Baptist conventions, where it included a much broader audience, and now has moved into local churches where the pain, in some ways, is more severe than it was at either the national or state levels. This revision of the 1994 book could not have come at a more appropriate time for many Baptist churches. It ought to be required reading for every pulpit search committee.

In his book, Humphreys describes the theology of the *old* Southern Baptist Convention, the theological SBC before 1979. He then proceeds to identify the *new* SBC, the theological SBC since 1979. In other words he describes "The Way We Were," before identifying "The Way We May Become," with all of its accompanying "lost traditions" and "innovations."

In one sense, Humphreys is a theological archivist, pointing to how Southern Baptists used to think. He then changes hats and becomes a theological prophet, not so much predicting the future as reading the signs of the times, seeing through what has happened to tell Southern Baptists where they are today. Writing insightfully of Southern Baptists, Humphreys says, "...our memory of who we once were is beginning to fade. Like people in a small boat sailing farther and farther from shore, we can no longer see the shoreline well enough to be certain where our journey began, so we are unable to interpret were we now are and where we are going."

Let me skip to the conclusion of the book and tell you that Humphreys, unlike some of us, is "still happy to continue to be a friend of the Convention." Nevertheless, he closes with a provocative question for all Southern Baptists. It is the question Governor Reagan asked President Carter in their famous 1980 presidential debate. The question for Southern Baptists: "Are you better off now than you were before 1979?" Humphreys acknowledges that "many fine Southern Baptists" believe they are better off. Unequivocatingly and tersely, Humphreys says, "I do not believe this." And then he tells you why. "I believe that the loss of...," but I am taking away all the fun. Read it for yourself.

Back during the Fundamentalist-Modernist controversy of the early twentieth century, fundamentalists published a twelve-volume paperback series designated *The Fundamentals*. Two wealthy laymen, Lyman and Milton Stewart, distributed three million copies free to Protestant ministers throughout America. I sincerely wish that some rich brothers or sisters, fundamentalist or moderate, conservative or liberal, would come forth today and pay to have *The Way We Were* sent to every Baptist in America.

And I do mean "every Baptist in America." While the book describes, what is for me, the sad and tragic theological unfolding of *Southern* Baptists for the last two decades of the twentieth century, *all* Baptists everywhere need to know what can happen to some of the

Baptist ideas and ideals, if not carefully guarded. If, however, my ficti-
tious wealthy brothers and sisters are not quite affluent enough to send
it to every "Baptist in America," they could merely restrict their free
gifts to every Baptist layperson and clergy in Southern Baptist
churches, people who constitute the target audience for the book.

I realize, of course, that all this stargazing about the distribution of
Fisher Humphreys's book is a far-fetched fancy conjured in a fevered
mind. Seriously, however, is it too much to hope that many Baptist
churches would purchase five to ten copies and circulate them among
the laity in their churches? Wiser money could not be spent for a local
Baptist church at this time in our denominational history. Wise pastors
could not do better than to teach this book, chapter by chapter, to
their people.

—Walter B. Shurden
Callaway Professor of Christianity
Executive Director, The Center for Baptist Studies
Mercer University, Macon, GA
4 October 2001

PREFACE
TO THE REVISED EDITION

For a decade and a half the Southern Baptist Convention was convulsed by a tragic controversy that inflicted appalling suffering upon tens of thousands of good people on both sides of the aisle. The conflict generated impassioned speech, as indeed it should; passion about the controversy was natural, appropriate, and necessary. But it was not sufficient. In this book I have attempted to write dispassionately about the controversy because I thought that I was losing sight of the trees in my passion for the forest and that others might be having the same experience. Who are the Southern Baptists? What do they believe? How are they changing? These are the questions I attempted to answer in this book.

The first edition of this book was published in 1995. In this second edition I have brought some of the statistics up to date, altered some phrasing in the first ten chapters, and rewritten the last two chapters, adding new information about the new leaders of the Convention and indicating changes in my own thinking.

I am indebted to my friend Bill Griffin for his encouragement while I was writing the first edition of this book. Four other friends read an earlier version of the book: Paul Basden, Timothy George, the late John Loftis, and Philip Wise. They provided helpful suggestions, and I am grateful to them all. Of course, the responsibility for any remaining misjudgments or asperities is mine.

I am indebted also to David Cassady and the other wonderful people at Smyth & Helwys for agreeing to publish a second edition of the book. In my judgment, Smyth & Helwys is playing an indispensable role in the life of Baptists in the South who do not share the vision of the new leaders of the Southern Baptist Convention.

I am dedicating this book to my home church, which in the space of only four years managed to instill in me as a teenager a profound respect for the theological heritage of the Southern Baptists, a respect that has lasted for four and a half decades. After I left Columbus, some of the men's Sunday school classes in the church made it possible for me to do graduate studies in theology, which I could not have done without their help, and my life took a turn which it otherwise might not. I am deeply grateful to them all. I am dedicating the book in particular to one couple in the church, Dr. S. B. Platt and his wife, the late Mrs. Clara Platt, who helped me to understand the inner meaning of the Baptist theological heritage, especially its commitment to missions, by the way they lived as well as by the things they said. They cannot know how much they contributed to my life.

> In essentials, unity.
> In non-essentials, liberty.
> In all things, charity.
>
> –*Rupertus Meldenius*[1]

Note

[1] *In necessariis unitas, in non necessariis libertas, in omnibus caritas.* This was first published in Rupertus Meldenius, *Paranaenesis Votiva pro Pace Ecclesiae* (Rottenburg, 1626), 62. "Rupertus Meldenius" is the pseudonym for an orthodox Lutheran theologian, probably Peter Meiderlin who died in Augsburg in 1651. Philip Schaff called these words "the motto of Christian Irenics." See Philip Schaff, *History of the Christian Church* (Grand Rapids: Wm. B. Eerdmans Publishing Company, 1974 [1910]), VII, 650-652. See also Carl Bertheau, "Meldenius, Rupertus" in *The New Schaff-Herzog Encyclopedia of Religious Knowledge* edited by Samuel Macauley Jackson, VII (Grand Rapids: Baker Book House, 1968), 287.

A FADING HERITAGE

The Southern Baptists

In 2000 there were approximately 281 million people living in the United States. The largest religious body in the country is the Roman Catholic church, with approximately 62 million members. The second largest is the Southern Baptist Convention, with approximately 16 million members. The 16 million Southern Baptists are members of approximately 41,000 churches. While the center of gravity for Southern Baptists is still the South, churches affiliated with the Convention are to be found in all fifty states and in the District of Columbia.

Southern Baptists operate the largest religious publishing house in the world, LifeWay Christian Resources, in Nashville. LifeWay Christian Resources, in turn, owns and operates 100 bookstores, the largest chain of religious bookstores in the nation. Southern Baptists have two mission boards, one for missionaries abroad and one for missionaries in the United States, with a total of about 10,000 missionaries under appointment. The Convention owns six seminaries, including three of the four largest accredited seminaries in the world, with a total enrollment of about 10,000 students.

The operations of the national organization constitute only a part of what Southern Baptists are doing. The 41,000 churches also are organized into forty state conventions, and many of these own and operate institutions of their own. For example, forty-five Baptist colleges and universities are affiliated in various ways with the different state conventions, including Baylor, Richmond, Wake Forest, Mercer, Stetson, and Samford.[1]

Although the growth rate of Southern Baptists has slowed in recent years, the Convention is still growing more rapidly than other large Protestant denominations in this country. Of denominations with more than a million members in the United States, only the Assemblies of God are growing faster than the Southern Baptists. But all is not well with the Southern Baptists. Since 1979 they have been engaged in a controversy. As a result the Southern Baptists are polarized into two groups, and all of the leaders of Southern Baptist agencies before 1979 have been replaced by new leaders. Even the naming of the two groups has been a matter of controversy. Those who approve of the new directions in the Convention tend to refer to the new leaders as "conservatives" and to the old leaders as "liberals." Those who disapprove of the new directions tend to call the new leaders "fundamentalists" and the old leaders "moderates" or, also, "conservatives."

The two groups do agree on one thing, however; they agree that Southern Baptists will never again be exactly the kind of people they were before the controversy. That is the premise upon which this book has been written: The Southern Baptists are changing and will not become again exactly the people they were before 1979. My primary purpose in writing this book is to record and interpret the beliefs that the Southern Baptists held in the years leading up to the controversy. I intend the book to be an archive of the way we were, theologically. My subsidiary purpose is to track the directions in which theology is moving in the new Southern Baptist Convention.

What Is the Relevance of This Archive?

Future historians who study American Christianity may well welcome a record of the beliefs that the Southern Baptists held before the controversy changed them, but is there anyone now who needs such a record? I believe there is. We who are Southern Baptists, or who think of ourselves as former Southern Baptists, are finding it difficult to interpret exactly what is happening to us, and one reason is that our memory of who we once were is beginning to fade. Like people in a small boat sailing farther and farther from shore, we can no longer see the shoreline well enough to be certain where our journey began, so we are unable to interpret where we now are and where we are going. Our origin should be for us a fixed point, so that we can better understand what is happening to us.

The changes in the theology of the Southern Baptists are also relevant to people who are not Southern Baptists. For example, in the years leading up to 1979, Southern Baptists were enthusiastic supporters of a rigorous separation of church and state. Like many Americans, they were at first puzzled by the Supreme Court decisions in the 1960s that determined that state-sponsored prayers in public schools constituted a violation of the no-establishment clause of the First Amendment, but many Southern Baptists quickly came to see that these decisions were consistent with the long-standing Baptist support for complete government neutrality toward religion. The new leaders of the Southern Baptists have indicated, however, that they do not see things that way. The Southern Baptist change of direction on this issue is important to all Americans.

I hope that this book will help readers understand what Southern Baptists once believed, so that they may understand better the changes taking place in the Convention and how the Convention today is different from the Convention before 1979.

Is an Archive Possible?

Scholars who study religions routinely expect to find several factors in the religions they study. Among these are a cult, a code, and a creed. A cult is a set of worship practices. A code is a set of moral rules. A creed is a set of beliefs, a worldview. The Southern Baptist Convention may therefore be expected to have these three. This book is about the third factor, the beliefs of the Southern Baptists. What worldview do these 16 million people share?

Some readers may be surprised to learn that the conventional wisdom among many of the scholars who study the Southern Baptist Convention has been that it is not possible to provide a description of the theological beliefs of Southern Baptists.

Three objections have been offered to the attempt to delineate the theology of the Southern Baptists. The first objection is that Baptists in general, and Southern Baptists in particular, have no written creed. Without a creed, the argument goes, we cannot know what the people believe. It is true that Southern Baptists do not have a creed. But they do have a confession, titled *The Baptist Faith and Message*. The version of this document that was adopted at the annual meeting of the Convention in 1963 provides a useful description of the beliefs of

Southern Baptists at that time; revisions made in 1998 and 2000 pro-vide indications of some of the concerns of the new leaders of the Convention.

A second argument used by those who believe that it is impossible to describe the theology of the Southern Baptists appeals to a famous Baptist slogan, "No creed but the Bible."[2] Since Southern Baptists are committed to the Bible as the source of their beliefs, the argument goes, the only possible description of their beliefs is the Bible itself. The premise is correct, but the conclusion does not follow. The argument overlooks an important fact, namely, that Southern Baptists believe that the Bible teaches some particular things. We here stipulate that throughout this book our description of the theology of the Southern Baptists is, in fact, a description of what the Southern Baptists believe the Bible teaches, for the Southern Baptists certainly think that their beliefs are biblical beliefs.

Finally, some scholars have felt that the beliefs held by 16 million Southern Baptists are too diverse to be susceptible of a single descrip-tion. Folk wisdom expresses this with a slogan: "Where there are two Southern Baptists, there are three opinions." Once again, the premise is correct but the conclusion does not follow. Let us here stipulate that a great diversity of beliefs exists among the Southern Baptists. But along with the diversity there is great unity. In the present book we shall describe and interpret the unity and the variety of the beliefs of the Southern Baptists.

Is There a Need for This Archive?

Even though they have no creeds, Baptists have left a paper trail that may be followed by those who wish to discern the shape of their theol-ogy.[3] In view of that paper trail, is there any need for a book such as this one? My conviction is that there is, because of the nature of the paper trail.

The trail is very large and very scattered. We have already noted that it includes *The Baptist Faith and Message* in its various editions. It also includes several editions of *The Baptist Hymnal*. Of course, Southern Baptists are not required either to believe *The Baptist Faith and Message* or to sing from *The Baptist Hymnal*, but, in fact, many Southern Baptist churches do use the hymnal and many Southern Baptist people believe much of what is in *The Baptist Faith and Message*.

The paper trail includes many other books. For example, in 1977 the Church Training Department of the Sunday School Board (now LifeWay Christian Resources) initiated a new study for the churches, called the Doctrine Study. Each year a Southern Baptist author has written a book on a particular doctrine, and the book has been widely distributed and studied in the churches. The authors have included pastors, denominational leaders, missionaries, and professors at colleges and seminaries. These books are a useful record of the theology of Southern Baptists. Another set of books that bridges the work of academic theologians with the consensus theology of the people is the 16-volume _Layman's Library of Christian Doctrine_, written by Southern Baptist pastors and professors and published in the 1980s.

The paper trail includes books of systematic theology and biblical theology written by professional Southern Baptist theologians.[4] It also includes the following: curriculum materials prepared for Sunday school and other church programs; articles that have appeared in the theological journals published by the seminaries;[5] many theological editorials and articles that have been printed in the thirty-nine newspapers published by the state conventions; and numerous articles, books, and doctoral dissertations written on the theology of Southern Baptist individuals and groups.[6]

A distinction needs to be made between the consensual theology of Southern Baptist people and the intentional, creative reworking of that consensus by professional theologians. Our interest here is more with folk theology than with academic theology, with what is lived out in church, home, and marketplace rather than with what is written in the books of scholars. Southern Baptist theologians have stayed extremely close to the concerns of the people in the churches, closer perhaps than is the case with theologians in most other denominations, but they are responsive to the concerns of the academic discipline of theology as well, as indeed they should be.[7] Unfortunately, there are no detailed, scientific surveys about the beliefs of Southern Baptists upon which to draw, though sociologist Nancy Ammerman has done some work of this type.[8] It is regrettable that no oral history of Southern Baptist folk theology has been recorded.[9]

Another source for understanding the theology of the Southern Baptists are their practices. For example, Southern Baptist churches baptize by immersion into water, not by pouring or sprinkling. No written record of this practice would be found, for example, in *The Baptist Hymnal*, yet the uniform practice makes it clear that Baptists believe this is the normative mode of baptism, and it is appropriate to take their practice as evidence for their belief.

The present book is needed because the paper trail that tells about the theology of Southern Baptists is large and dispersed. The shape and texture of Southern Baptist theology before the controversy are fading and will fade from our memories; this retrieval of our fading heritage is offered to our children as a patrimony and to ourselves as a reminder of the way we were.

Interpreting the Controversy

The Southern Baptist Convention is a large and complex organization, and the controversy that began in 1979 is a large and complex social dislocation. Many interpretations of the Southern Baptist controversy have been offered. This is a good thing. Because the controversy is complex, many interpretations are needed.[10] We do not err when we embrace several interpretations; we err when we assume that a single interpretation tells us everything that is important about the controversy. For example, some well-intentioned interpreters have suggested that the controversy was "really" about political power; it was about political power, both inside and outside the Convention, but it was not about political power alone.

The interpreter also should not assume that theology is a smoke screen to cover other unmentionable issues such as sexism or racism; this seems to be the thesis of one study.[11] The problem with such a thesis is that it is unfalsifiable; nothing counts against it. When dealing with empirical matters one should be able to state with some precision what empirical data count against a proposed interpretation. The most helpful interpretations of a complex social movement such as the controversy in the Convention are those that attend to the complexities of the movement, report them with some fullness, and attempt to show the relationships among them. It is reductionism of the most egregious sort to assert that the theology of the Southern Baptists is "really" a cover for racism or sexism. This is like saying that romantic love is "really" only about sex or that capital punishment is "really" only about revenge.

Several major kinds of interpretation of the controversy are needed. For example, the controversy needs to be interpreted histori-cally[12] and sociologically.[13] It also needs to be understood in terms of the personalities who have led in the changes and those who have resisted it.[14] Interpreters who emphasize the history, sociology, and per-sonalities of the controversy give attention to many factors, including the expansion of Southern Baptists beyond the South; the cultural changes in the nation; the civil rights movement and the response of the South; the changing role of women in America; the development of Southern Baptist bureaucracies; the growth of the financial base of the Southern Baptists; the changes in American political life and the place of Baptists in those changes; the culture wars in America; the increasing influence of television upon church life; the worldwide resurgence of religious movements that bear a family resemblance to this one;[15] and many other factors.

To the interpretations of the controversy emphasizing history, soci-ology, and personalities, I want to add an interpretation that emphasizes theology. From the beginning of the controversy in 1979, the new leaders of the Convention have insisted that theology is one of their central concerns. I know of no reason to suppose either that they are insincere or that they are mistaken about their intentions, and in that sense, the controversy clearly is about theology. Furthermore, with hindsight it seems clear to many observers that, as a matter of fact, the-ology has been a factor in the controversy. As David Morgan has written, "The struggle was both a crusade for truth and a struggle for power."[16] Theology was an important issue in the controversy, but not the only issue. Was it the most important issue? I expect it was for some people and not for others. My assumption in this book is simply that the complex social dislocation called the controversy comprises many important components and that one of them is theology.

The Organization of This Book

This book is not a history of the Southern Baptists.[17] Nor is the format of the book a sequence of theological themes[18] or simply a review of beliefs peculiar to Baptists.[19] This book has three parts. The first is a review of the majority tradition accepted by most Southern Baptists until the controversy began. It is the *consensus fidelium*, the under-standing these Christians share about God, the world, and their place in the world. The second part is a review of six alternative agendas that have been offered to Southern Baptists, which significant minorities of Southern Baptists have accepted. These agendas could be called the *diversitas fidelium*, the diversity to be found among these Christians. The third part is an effort to interpret what is happening to the majority tradition as a result of the changes in the Convention since 1979. The new majority tradition could be called the *revisio fidelium*, the revised beliefs of the majority of the new Convention, or at least of its leaders.

The majority tradition is described in chapters one through four. In chapter 1 we review the beliefs that Southern Baptists share with all the Christians in the world. In Chapter 2 we consider the beliefs that Southern Baptists share with Protestant Christians. In Chapter 3 we review the beliefs that Southern Baptists share with other Baptists. And in Chapter 4 we examine the beliefs that Southern Baptists share with the churches that have accepted the orientation to Christianity developed during the great revivalist movement of the eighteenth century. The sequence is chronological:[20] a description is given of the beliefs of groups that originated in the first century, the sixteenth century, the seventeenth century, and the eighteenth century, respectively.

Six alternative agendas are proposed by minorities among Southern Baptists. These are described in chapters 5 through 10. They also are examined in chronological order. The first alternative agenda is the Anabaptist agenda, proposed to the church by the more radical wing of the Reformation. The second is the Calvinist agenda. These two traditions originated in Europe in the sixteenth century. The third agenda was the Landmark Baptist agenda, a distinctively American movement that developed during the nineteenth century. The fourth is the deeper life agenda, which developed in Great Britain and America during the nineteenth century in many Protestant churches. The fifth is the fundamentalist agenda, a distinctly American agenda that developed early in the twentieth century as a response to liberal Protestant theology. The sixth is the progressive agenda. Unlike the others, this is not a group of interrelated beliefs but rather several discrete beliefs that have been offered to Southern Baptists since the middle of the twentieth century.

The third part comprises two chapters. In the first I display which of the majority beliefs held in the years leading up to 1979 are at risk in the new Southern Baptist Convention. In the second I display which of the beliefs which were held by minority groups in 1979 are becoming part of the majority tradition in the new Convention.

Notes

[1]These universities retain ties to their state conventions, though the conventions no longer have complete control of them.

[2]The phrase apparently originated in the Churches of Christ, but the concept to which it points has been accepted by Southern Baptists throughout their history. Those who organized the Southern Baptist Convention in 1845 explained that they were not going to propose a creed for the Convention because of the "Baptist aversion to all creeds." See William L. Lumpkin, "The Nature and Authority of Baptist Confessions of Faith," *Review and Expositor* (Winter 1979), 25.

[3]Throughout this book I shall use the word "Baptists" to refer to Southern Baptists and to persons who think of themselves as erstwhile Southern Baptists. The context will make it clear if I intend anyone other than these people.

[4]In the twentieth century the list would include E. Y. Mullins, W. T. Conner, W. O. Carver, Frank Stagg, W. W. Stevens, Dale Moody, Dallas Roark, James Wm. McClendon, Morris Ashcraft, Frank Tupper, Warren McWilliams, A. J. Conyers, and Curtis Freeman, to name only a few. For a review of the work of Baptist theologians, see *Theologians of the Baptist Tradition*, edited by Timothy George and David S. Dockery (Nashville: Broadman & Holman, 2001).

[5]In the 1980s there were four of these: *Faith and Mission*, *Review and Expositor*, *Southwestern Journal of Theology*, and *The Theological Educator*. The first and last of these are no longer being published, and *Review and Expositor* is now published by an independent group rather than by a seminary faculty.

[6]Until the Southern Baptist Convention was reorganized in the late 1990s, it operated a small organization called The Historical Commission. This commission published a very important journal entitled *Baptist History and Heritage*; this journal is now published independently of the Convention by the Baptist History and Heritage Society.

[7]See *Has Our Theology Changed? Southern Baptist Thought since 1845*, Paul Basden, ed. (Nashville: Broadman & Holman, 1993). During the controversy one criticism made of professional theologians was that they were, in fact, too responsive to the academic discipline of theology and too unresponsive to the churches.

[8]Nancy Tatom Ammerman, *Baptist Battles: Social Change and Religious Conflict in the Southern Baptist Convention* (New Brunswick: Rutgers University Press, 1990).

[9]*Foxfire 7* (Garden City: Anchor Books, 1973, 1980, 1982), edited by Paul F. Gillespie, contains interviews with several Southern Baptist pastors in Appalachia. *The Theological Educator*, a journal published by the faculty of New Orleans Baptist Theological Seminary from 1967 until 1998, began in 1976 a series of interviews with Southern Baptist laypersons, pastors, missionaries, denominational leaders, and professors, on the topic of "Southern Baptist Theology Today." Other Southern Baptist leaders have been interviewed in newspapers and magazines.

[10]The need for multiple interpretations informs a book edited by Nancy Tatom Ammerman, *Southern Baptists Observed: Multiple Perspectives on a Changing Denomination* (Knoxville: University of Tennessee Press, 1993).

[11]Ellen M. Rosenberg, *The Southern Baptists: A Subculture in Transition* (Knoxville: The University of Tennessee Press, 1989).

[12]Claude L. Howe, Jr., has written two excellent articles that summarize the events in the controversy: "From Houston to Dallas" and "From Dallas to New Orleans." These articles were published in *The Theological Educator* (Spring 1990). In my judgment the best books interpreting the controversy historically are *God's Last and Only Hope: The Fragmentation of the Southern Baptist Convention* by Bill J. Leonard (Grand Rapids: William B. Eerdmans, 1990) and *The New Crusades, the New Holy Land: Conflict in the Southern Baptist Convention, 1969–1991* by David T. Morgan (Tuscaloosa: The University of Alabama Press, 1996). A very influential background study is "The 1980–81 Carver-Barnes Lectures" by Walter B. Shurden (Wake Forest: Southeastern Baptist Theological Seminary, 1980). For a history of the development of moderate institutions see *The Struggle for the Soul of the SBC*, Walter B. Shurden, ed. (Macon GA: Mercer University Press, 1993); in it Shurden provides a summary of the major events in the controversy.

[13]The best sociological interpretation of the controversy known to me is *Baptist Battles: Social Change and Religious Conflict in the Southern Baptist Convention* by Nancy Tatom Ammerman (New Brunswick: Rutgers University Press, 1990).

[14]Many books tell about the personalities in the controversy. The indispensable insider's view is *What Happened to the Southern Baptist Convention?: A Memoir of the Controversy* by Grady C. Cothen (Macon GA: Smyth & Helwys Publishing, 1993). James C. Hefley began in 1986 a series of books titled *The Truth in Crisis* (Hannibal MO: Hannibal Books, 1986 seq.) which is full of information about personalities and events. Also see *A Hill on Which to Die: One Southern Baptist's Journey*, Paul Pressler (Nashville: Broadman & Holman, 1999) and *The Baptist Reformation: The Conservative Resurgence in the Southern Baptist Convention*, Jerry Sutton (Nashville: Broadman & Holman, 2000). Joe Edward Barnhart's *The Southern Baptist Holy War: The Self-Destructive Struggle for Power within the Largest Protestant Denomination in America* (Austin: Texas Monthly Press, 1986) has some valuable vignettes. The cast of players is described in *The Takeover in the Southern Baptist Convention*, edited by Rob James (Decatur GA: SBC Today, 1989; there are several editions of this booklet that was originally the report of a committee of a local congregation in Richmond). Both the church press and the public press have carried hundreds of stories about the controversy; *SBC Today*, now called *Baptists Today*, is especially helpful. See also David Morgan, "Upheaval in the Southern Baptist Convention, 1979–1990, The Texas Connection," *Perspectives in Religious Studies* (Spring 1992).

[15]One of the most exhaustive studies of religion ever made is called "The Fundamentalism Project." See Martin E. Marty and R. Scott Appleby, eds., *Fundamentalisms Observed* (Chicago: University of Chicago Press, 1991).

[16]David T. Morgan, *The New Crusades, the New Holy Land*, ix.

[17]There seem to have been few efforts to write a history of Southern Baptist theology. A recent one was *Winds of Doctrine: The Origin and Development of Southern Baptist Theology*, W. Wiley Richards (Lanham MD: University Press of America, 1991). Richards offers the interesting proposal that the theology of the Southern Baptists began as Calvinistic evangelicalism, became in the nineteenth century ecclesiastical evangelicalism,

from 1900 to 1960 was evangelistic evangelicalism, and since 1960 has been engaged in a struggle to see whether it will continue as neo-orthodox evangelicalism or as inerrancy evangelicalism. With much of this I agree, though the issue since 1960, it seems to me, might be better expressed as whether Southern Baptists will continue as evangelistic/missionary evangelicals or be transformed into inerrancy evangelicals; and the transformation is decidedly under way.

[18]Such books are available. For example, Herschel H. Hobbs, the chairman of the committee that revised *The Baptist Faith and Message* in 1963, has written a commentary on that document. See his *The Baptist Faith and Message* (Nashville: Convention Press, 1971). *What Southern Baptists Believe* (Louisville: Park Hurst Publishers, 1988) by Hankins Parker is also a running commentary on the theological themes developed in *The Baptist Faith and Message*.

[19]"The Southern Baptist Alliance Covenant" is an example of a document that seems to have been designed to emphasize, among other things, distinctively Baptist beliefs. It is the confessional document of The Southern Baptist Alliance, now called The Alliance of Baptists. See *Being Baptist Means Freedom*, Alan Neely, ed. (Charlotte: Southern Baptist Alliance, 1988).

[20]If the sequence moved from the largest group (all Christians) to the smallest group, then the sequence would be all Christians, Protestant Christians, revivalist Christians, and Baptist Christians.

PART ONE

THE
MAJORITY
TRADITION

CHAPTER 1

BELIEFS BAPTISTS SHARE WITH ALL CHRISTIANS

The followers of Jesus Christ in the world today are found in thousands of churches and denominations, and the initial impression of an observer is one of variety to the point of dissipation. An interested bystander might well ask, "Do these people share any common beliefs?" Even if we discover that they do, will not their shared beliefs be, so to speak, a lowest common denominator, a collection of ideas which are agreed upon only because they are so trivial that no one cares enough about them to disagree about them?

These natural assumptions are held by many people who observe churches casually and by some who study the churches carefully. But they should not be held, for they are not true. In fact, the beliefs held by all the churches are religiously the most indispensable and theologically the most profound. These universal Christian beliefs may be summarized by considering eleven themes.

There Is One God

Jews, Christians, and Muslims agree concerning the first of these beliefs, namely, that there is only one true God. There were brushes with monotheism before it became the cardinal doctrine of the Hebrew people. Ikhnaton promoted it in Egypt, and in the fourth century before Christ. Plato, Aristotle, and other Greek philosophers came to see that the Ultimate Reality must be one rather than many. What is remarkable is not that these precursors of Hebrew monotheism arose, but that they failed, and that monotheism as held by the Jews succeeded so fully that it now is an operating assumption for Western philosophy and theology and has credibility even in some Eastern religions. For example, in the West there is a vigorous discussion of the

arguments for and against the existence of God; there is no discussion
of arguments for or against the existence of gods. Moreover, in
Hinduism many intellectuals such as the late philosopher and president of India, Sarvepalli Radhakrishnan, believe that the many gods
and avatars of Hinduism are different names for a single deity.

Monotheism has not always been so dominant. When Israel
became monotheistic, she was alone and her neighbors thought she
was foolish. Her neighbors asked, "Where is your God?" (Ps 115:2).
Not surprisingly, scholars have disagreed about exactly when the
Hebrew people became monotheists. Some have thought that
monotheism was the original belief of humankind and that polytheism
was a later corruption. Others have seen Abraham as the first
monotheist. Others have asserted that Moses was the first monotheist,
in part because the Shema is attributed to him: "Hear, O Israel, the
Lord our God is one Lord" (Deut 6:4). More critical scholars have
argued that monotheism did not come into its own until the great
prophets of the eighth and seventh centuries before Christ.[1]

Our interest here is not in the chronology of monotheism but in
the fact that the conviction that there is only one true God became
the cardinal belief of the Hebrews. From the beginning, monotheism
was fully accepted by all Christians. It is true that the Christian doctrine of the Trinity goes beyond Hebrew monotheism, but it is an
addition to, not a rejection of, monotheism. The Shema is quoted in
the New Testament (Mark 12:2), always with approval, and some of
the early Christian confessions of faith such as Ephesians 4:4-6 assert
that there is only one God.

Monotheism is one of the great success stories of the Jewish and
Christian religions. Most people in the West find it superfluous to
affirm the conviction that there is only one true God; this belief is too
self-evident to need to be asserted or defended. This is as true of
Baptists as it is of all other Christians. Article II of *The Baptist Faith and
Message* says simply: "There is one and only one living and true God."[2]

God Created the World

The second belief that Baptists share with all other Christians is the
belief that God created the world. Like monotheism, this belief has
become part of the thinking of most Western people. Ask people in the
West, "What do you think of when I say the word 'God'?" and most
will respond, "The One who made the world." Yet it is by no means

self-evident that God created the world. Other relationships between God and the world are, in principle, quite possible. For example, Plato taught that the world is as eternal as God is; God shapes the world but did not create it. The Stoics taught that the world is God's body, and God is the soul of the world. Some Gnostics taught that the world was created not by God but by a being that had emanated from God.

Christians, like Jews and Muslims, believe that God is the creator of the world because this truth is revealed in the Bible. The placing of the story of Creation at the very beginning of the Bible, Genesis 1–2, reinforces the importance of the idea. The Hebrew Scriptures contain other passages that affirm God as Creator, such as Job 38–39, Psalm 104, and Isaiah 45:9-12. The New Testament reaffirms creation when it says that God "brings into being what did not exist" and when it tells us that "it is by faith that we understand that the universe was created by God's Word, so that what can be seen was made out of what cannot be seen" (Rom 4:17; Heb 11:3).

In the ancient world, the affirmation that God is the Creator of all things was an alternative to views that originated in other religions. In the early history of the church, the belief that God is the Creator was an alternative to views that originated in philosophy. In the modern world, belief in God as Creator has been presented as an alternative to views that originate in science.

Because of the different stances Christians take toward the issue of how God created the world, it is easy to lose sight of the universal agreement among Christians that God is the Creator of all things. In particular, Christians disagree among themselves about the accounts of the age of the universe offered by some scientific theories, and they disagree about whether to accept scientific hypotheses concerning the evolution of life on this planet. These differences are important, but it is much more important that, however much Christians may disagree about how God created the world, there is no disagreement about the fact that God did create the world.

Southern Baptists, of course, agree with other Christians that God created the world. *The Baptist Faith and Message* (II) says that God is the "Creator, Redeemer, Preserver, and Ruler of the universe." Southern Baptists sing praise to "the King of Creation" who "o'er all things so wondrously reigneth," and they are confident that "This is my Father's world."

Since God created human beings, that means that human beings are good. The Creation story in Genesis speaks of five ways in which human beings are unique: they are created last, they are created in God's image, God breathes into them the breath of life, they are given dominion over the rest of the creation, and after God created them God said that it was "very good." In all of literature there may be no finer passage about the dignity of human beings than is found in Psalm 8:

> When I look at the sky, which you have made, at the moon and the stars, which you set in their places — what is man, that you think of him; mere man, that you care for him? Yet you made him inferior only to yourself; you crowned him with glory and honor. You appointed him ruler over everything you made; you placed him over all creation.

The World Is a Fallen World

The story of the fall of the world into sin, like the story of the creation of the world, is placed early in the Bible (Gen 3), and that has contributed to sin's being a dominant theme in the theology of Christians. What Genesis affirms by the memorable story of the Garden of Eden, the Bible reaffirms many times in later stories of the sins and failures of individuals, of the nation Israel, and of the Christian church. Perhaps no other narratives in the world are so candid about the failures of their central personalities as are those in the Bible; except for Jesus himself, every major character in the Bible is presented "warts and all," and the emphasis often falls on the warts. The Bible also affirms the sin of the human race in non-narrative terms in passages such as Romans 1–2.

The Christian church has inherited this realistic vision of the human predicament and has affirmed it repeatedly. It is a vision that is sometimes resented by people as too gloomy and pessimistic, and doubtless there have been times when the church emphasized the grimness of the human predicament to the neglect of Christian hope. But the realism of the Bible about sin is very reassuring to those who wonder if it is possible to be realistic about the human problem and still retain hope.

Christians have interpreted the sin problem in different ways. In Israel the great prophets such as Amos encountered people who worried too much about the details of religious rituals and too little about the great issues of the moral law, and Jesus found himself in controversy with people who kept the letter but violated the spirit of the law. Both of these issues continue today, and others have surfaced in the church's history. Despite the variety of interpretations, however, there is considerable agreement among Christians about the human predicament. For example, Christians see the source of the human problem, not in ignorance, suffering, or death, but in sin. Here is how *The Baptist Faith and Message* (III) expresses it:

> By his free choice man sinned against God and brought sin into the human race. Through the temptation of Satan man transgressed the command of God, and fell from his original innocence; whereby his posterity inherit a nature and an environment inclined toward sin, and as soon as they are capable of moral action become transgressors and are under condemnation.

As this quotation makes clear, Southern Baptists are aware of the social dimension of sin. However, they tend to emphasize the personal aspect of sin more than the social. Sin is fundamentally an individual's act of moral disobedience to the law of God, which brings upon the sinner the righteous judgment of God. One of the Baptists' favorite hymns, "Amazing Grace," speaks of the human predicament this way: "Amazing grace! How sweet the sound / That saved a wretch like me. / I once was lost, but now am found, / Was blind, but now I see."

One of the most extraordinary achievements of Christian doctrine is its success in balancing the belief that human beings are good because they are created by God with the belief that they are hopelessly lost in sin. This subtle combination of ideas is held, not only by intellectuals in the church, but by unschooled Christians, and even by children. The balance between these two beliefs has practical consequences. For example, is the Christian understanding of human beings optimistic or pessimistic? Is it realistic or idealistic?

It is optimistic because it affirms that the world is God's good creation and that human beings are the crowning work of God's creation, made in God's own image, only a little lower than God. It also is realistic because it affirms that the world is hopelessly fallen away from its true destiny, and that human beings are enslaved by evil powers and forces, both internal and external, from which they cannot deliver themselves. Blaise Pascal captured well the paradox of the Christian vision of human beings when he wrote:

> What sort of a freak then is man! How novel, how monstrous, how chaotic, how paradoxical, how prodigious! Judge of all things, feeble earthworm, repository of truth, sink of doubt and error, glory and refuse of the universe! Who will unravel such a tangle?[3]

Yet, the final Christian word is one of hope rather than despair, for the Christian message is an affirmation that God does for sinners what they cannot do for themselves; God rescues them from their sin.

God Is Father, Son, and Holy Spirit

The word "Trinity" does not appear in the Bible, nor does it appear in *The Baptist Faith and Message*, but the Trinitarian understanding of God is presented in both. The second article of *The Baptist Faith and Message* is titled simply "God," and it comprises three parts: "God the Father," "God the Son," and "God the Holy Spirit." These categories may seem scholastic to outsiders, but they are living realities to Southern Baptists just as they are to other Christians.

Further, the religious life of Christians is probably more Trinitarian than their theology. Christians worship and believe in God, whom they think of and pray to as the Father of Jesus Christ and as their own heavenly Father. They also are religiously committed to Jesus as Lord and Savior, in whom they have placed their faith and hope for salvation. They also very much believe in the Holy Spirit as the presence of God with the church and with individual Christians, and they know that the Spirit's work is indispensable to their faith and life. Baptists, like all Christians, are Trinitarian in their common religious life. *The Baptist Faith and Message* makes this fact clear, while displaying the reticence to speak directly about the Trinity that also is characteristic of the Bible.

Yet Baptists do speak about the Trinity. For example, they proclaim as gospel the story of the crucifixion and resurrection of Christ; they say that Christ thereby reconciled sinners to God; and they teach that those who accept this message receive the gift of the Holy Spirit (see Acts 2:22-40, especially v. 33). Also, they follow the baptismal formula of Matthew 28:19-20 and baptize "in the name of the Father, and of the Son, and of the Holy Spirit." These verses are a favorite text of

Baptists who refer to them as "The Great Commission." Again, Baptists sing more than fifteen hymns and doxologies that are Trinitarian and are found in *The Baptist Hymnal.* Some of these hymns devote one verse each to the Father, the Son, and the Spirit. Here, for example, are the opening lines of the four verses of one popular hymn: "Come, thou Almighty King / Come, thou Incarnate Word / Come, Holy Comforter / To thee, great One in Three." Baptists certainly know what the word "Trinity" means, and some of them have definite ideas about the Trinity. Nevertheless, the strength of their commitment to the Trinitarian understanding of God is measured best not by their articulation of their belief, but by its occurrence in the practices of the church such as gospel preaching, baptism, and the singing of hymns.

The Father Sent the Son into the World

The fifth belief that Baptists share with all Christians is sometimes called "Incarnation" and is discussed by scholars in terms of "Christology." Baptists tend not to use these two terms often. They employ much more frequently the biblical language of the Father "sending" the Son into the world. It is almost certainly the case that the most loved verse in the Bible among Baptists is John 3:16: "For God so loved the world that he gave his only-begotten Son." Baptists recognize that the coming of the Son of God into the world is surrounded by mystery, but they accept, as the Christian church always has, that his mysterious coming was by means of a virgin mother. The fact is celebrated unself-consciously in Christmas carols and in Christmas pageants in Baptist churches each year; it has never been seriously debated among Southern Baptists. Baptists do not share the devotion to Mary that many other Christians have, but they share the belief of all other Christians that Mary was a virgin.

Most Southern Baptist churches do not employ creeds as a part of their liturgy, and many Southern Baptist people are not familiar with the Apostles' Creed.[4] It is interesting to note, therefore, that *The Baptist Faith and Message*(II) employs the language of the Apostles' Creed when speaking of the birth of Christ. It says: "In His incarnation as Jesus Christ he was conceived of the Holy Spirit and born of the virgin Mary."

Jesus Lived, Preached, Taught, Loved, Died, and Rose Again to Save the World

Jesus Christ stands at the center of the Christian faith. The four gospels are stories about his life and work. The gospel message is the story of his death and resurrection. Here is how the apostle Paul summarized the gospel: "I passed on to you what I received, which is of the greatest importance: that Christ died for our sins, as written in the Scriptures; that he was buried and that he was raised to life three days later, as written in the Scriptures" (1 Cor 15:3-4).

Baptists love the story of Jesus, as all Christians do. They confess their faith in it in *The Baptist Faith and Message*, and they sing about it in hymns such as "One Day," "Tell Me the Story of Jesus," and "Victory in Jesus": "I heard about his healing / Of his cleansing power revealing / How he made the lame to walk again / And caused the blind to see; / And then I cried 'dear Jesus, / Come and heal my broken spirit,' / And somehow Jesus came and brought / to me the victory."

For Baptists as for Paul, the emphasis falls upon the death and resurrection of Christ rather than upon his life and teachings, but the stories of his life and teachings are loved and told over and over by Baptists. Baptists preach that Christ died and rose again to save sinners; the message of salvation through Christ is the central feature of Baptist preaching. *The Baptist Faith and Message* (II) says: "In his death on the cross He made provision for the redemption of men from sin." The created world is a stage on which the drama of redemption is acted out, and the story of Jesus is the center of that drama. The optimism of the Baptist message originates not in any observations about the world or general theories about progress, but in the conviction that "God was in Christ, reconciling the world unto himself" (2 Cor 5:19, KJV).

The Father and the Son Poured Out the Holy Spirit on the Church

In Acts 2 Luke tells the story of God giving the Holy Spirit to the disciples of Christ on the Day of Pentecost. The gift of the Spirit fulfilled several prophecies in the Hebrew Scriptures and also fulfilled promises that Jesus had made to his disciples.[5] When the Spirit was given, the church was born. One of God's most precious gifts to the church is God's presence with them as Holy Spirit. Baptists believe in the Holy

Spirit. *The Baptist Faith and Message* (II) lists sixteen activities of the Spirit. The Spirit enables people to understand the Bible, cultivates Christian character, comforts believers, gives spiritual gifts to Christians, protects and assures Christians, and enlightens and empowers the Christian and the church in worship, evangelism, and service.

Baptists sing about the Spirit less frequently than they do about Christ, but their hymns include prayers for the power, cleansing, enlightenment, and comfort of the Spirit. Most Southern Baptists have avoided the Pentecostal and charismatic movements, but they believe very deeply in the presence and work of the Spirit.

The Spirit Guides and Empowers the Church on Its World Mission

The Christian church is a missionary church. It was born to do missionary work, as the Book of Acts emphasizes. Southern Baptists love to emphasize this aspect of the church's work. Mission is the *raison d'etre* of Southern Baptists. Those who founded the Southern Baptist Convention thought of themselves as "organizing a plan for eliciting, combining, and directing the energies of the whole denomination in one sacred effort, for the propagation of the Gospel."[6]

Baptists sing about missions. "We've a Story to Tell to the Nations," they sing. They tell their youth that their responsibility with reference to the gospel is to "Pass It On."

More than seventy percent of the money given through the central funding agency of the Southern Baptist Convention, called the Cooperative Program, is given to the two mission boards. Further, two very large offerings are taken in Baptist churches each year, one at Christmas for foreign missions and one at Easter for missions work in the United States; together they amount to more than $150 million a year. Southern Baptists are serious about missions, and their commitment to missions has been the strongest bond holding them together across the decades.

Baptists recognize that, for all their plans and all their energy and commitment, the success of the missionary enterprise depends on God's blessing it, and they know that God's blessing is given through the Holy Spirit who guides and empowers the church in this work. It is the Holy Spirit who "calls men to the savior, and effects regeneration" (*The Baptist Faith and Message*, II).

The Church Preaches the Gospel
and Observes the Ordinances of Christ

From its inception, the Christian church was a preaching church. The book of Acts contains summaries of sermons preached by Peter, Stephen, and Paul. The content of the apostolic preaching was the kerygma, the message that Christ had died and risen again to bring salvation. The church is a community of memory that never forgets what happened on Good Friday and Easter Sunday. The Christian church is reminded of the momentous events of Jesus' life not only by its preachers, but by its observance of two symbolic acts, baptism and the Lord's Supper. From its inception, in obedience to commands given by Christ, the church baptized and observed the Lord's Supper.[7] Southern Baptists believe in preaching, and they believe in baptism and the Lord's Supper.

Most Southern Baptist churches have three services each week, two on Sunday and a third on Wednesday evening, with a sermon as part of each one. Many churches still follow the traditional practice of setting aside one or more periods of time each year for special revival preaching. Many Baptists also listen to other preaching, either on the radio or television or by attending special services at nearby churches. Preaching is an important factor in the life of Southern Baptists.

Baptists get their name from one of the two principal church ordinances; *ordinance* is the name Southern Baptists ordinarily used for what most churches call *sacraments*, namely, baptism and the Lord's Supper. Surprisingly, however, Southern Baptists tend not to think of the observance of the ordinances as a component of the mission of the church. Rather, they think of the observance of the ordinances as acts of obedience to Christ oberved by the church when the primary work of preaching, evangelizing, and missions has been carried out. The phrase "Word and Sacrament," which is so familiar in many churches, is rarely used by Baptists.

God Will Complete This Work in the Future

From its inception Christianity was a religion of hope. The earliest Christians had been trained to hope by their Jewish faith, and Jesus had given them a reason to hope by means of his message and also by his resurrection from the dead. Christians look not only to a past in which God has acted in history but to a future in which God will complete history. They think of God as pushing them from behind, and as with them in the present moment, and as waiting for them in the future.

Southern Baptists share the hope which has characterized the life of the church from the beginning. Generally they speak of this hope in terms of heaven; there are eighteen hymns in *The Baptist Hymnal* about heaven. Some of the titles are "We're Marching to Zion," "O That Will Be Glory for Me," "When We All Get to Heaven," and "Face to Face with Christ My Savior." *The Baptist Faith and Message* says simply: "The righteous in their resurrected and glorified bodies will receive their reward and will dwell forever in Heaven with the Lord."

Baptists believe that salvation includes many things, and they can speak eloquently of these sayings. To be saved is to find a meaning for life; it is to find a true Friend, Jesus Christ; it is to be forgiven of our sins; it is to become part of the family of God. But most of all, to be saved is to have your eternal destiny changed from hell to heaven. Evangelistic preaching often takes the form of warnings about hell, and heaven figures much larger in Baptist theology than even the numerous hymns might suggest. Baptist hope is not restricted to heaven, however; Baptists have ideas about the future of life on this planet. They hold diverse ideas about this, so it is quite appropriate that *The Baptist Faith and Message* (X) uses the following neutral phrasing: "God, in His own time and in His own way, will bring the world to its appropriate end." The diversity of beliefs about how the world will end should not distract our attention from the more fundamental fact, which is that Baptists share with all Christians the conviction that they are entitled to live in hope because the future belongs to God, just as the past and the present do.

The Bible Tells Us This Wonderful Story

The Bible is the holy book of the Christian church. The earliest Christians treasured the Hebrew Scriptures, in which they found many passages that helped them to understand God's great work of sending Jesus Christ and pouring out the Spirit. Soon Christians began to write their own books, and, under the leadership of God, they collected them and eventually recognized them as also being the Word of God, authoritative for the faith and life of the Christian community.

Baptists are proud to be a people of the Book, the Bible. They owe their existence to the efforts of women and men in the seventeenth century who felt that it was important to leave the Church of England in order to form a church that would be more faithful to the New Testament. Baptists study the Bible, read the Bible, teach the Bible, preach the Bible, argue about the Bible, and write about the Bible. They even sing about the Bible: "Holy Bible, book divine, precious treasure, thou art mine." In the summer study program called Vacation Bible School that Baptists (and many other churches) conduct for children, the children usually participate in a pledge to the American flag, a pledge to the Christian flag, and a pledge to the Bible. Baptists share the conviction of all Christians that the Bible is the Word of God. Baptists love the Bible because, as a beloved hymn says, "Beyond the sacred page, / I seek thee, Lord / My spirit pants for thee, / O living Word." The Bible has the "wonderful words of life" that Baptists need and that they proclaim to all who will listen.

The Baptist Faith and Message (I) affirms clearly the convictions of Baptists about the Bible, that it is God's Word, that it is uniquely inspired, and that it is authoritative for the faith and life of the church: "The Holy Bible was written by men divinely inspired and is the record of God's revelation of Himself to man. It is a perfect treasure of divine instruction. It has God for its author, salvation for its end, and truth, without any mixture of error, for its matter." Since 1979 Southern Baptists have been engaged in a controversy about the Bible, but the controversy has not been about the ideas mentioned here: that the Bible is God's Word, that it is uniquely inspired, and that it is authoritative for the faith and life of the church. The controversy has been about a more technical issue than these, and we will deal with that issue in chapter nine. For now, it is important to note that the Bible is the holy book for Baptists as it is for other Christians and that Baptists, like other Christians, regard it as God's Word and as the written authority for the faith and life of the church.

These, then, are eleven beliefs that Southern Baptists hold in common with all of the world's Christians, whether Protestant, Catholic, or Eastern Orthodox: there is one God; God created the world; the world is fallen; God is Father, Son, and Spirit; the Father sent the Son into the world; Christ lived and died and rose again to save the world; the Father and the Son gave their Spirit to the church; the Spirit guides and empowers the church on its world mission; the mission includes preaching and the ordinances; God will complete this work in the future; and the Bible tells us this wonderful story. The conventional name for these beliefs shared by all Christians is "Christian orthodoxy." They are what has been believed everywhere, always, by everyone in the church.[8] They are the beliefs to which C. S. Lewis referred as "mere Christianity."

Southern Baptists are orthodox Christians. These eleven beliefs are the most important beliefs that Southern Baptists hold. In my judgment, they are a highest common denominator, not a lowest. What unites Baptists and other Christians is far more important than what divides them. All Christians do not share this judgment. In fact, the center of gravity in the faith and life of many Southern Baptists lies not in what has been described in this chapter, but in some of the beliefs described in Chapter 4. Nevertheless, the beliefs described in this chapter are the indispensable background for those revivalist beliefs.

Notes

[1]Isaiah 40–66 is explicitly monotheistic; see, for example, Isaiah 45:5.

[2]Throughout this book references to *The Baptist Faith and Message* are to the 1963 edition unless otherwise stated.

[3]Blaise Pascal, *Pensées*, 131, translated by A. J. Krailsheimer (London: Penguin Books, 1966), 65.

[4]Other Baptists are more familiar with the Apostles' Creed. For example, at the first meeting of the Baptist World Alliance, held in London in 1905, Alexander Maclaren of Great Britain led his fellow Baptists to stand together and recite the Apostles' Creed.

[5]See, for example, Joel 2 and Luke 11:11-13.

[6]Quoted in *Meet Southern Baptists*, Albert McClellen (Nashville: Broadman Press, 1978), 29-30.

[7]Christ commands the church to baptize in Matthew 28:19-20, and to observe the Lord's Supper in Matthew 26:26-27. Luke tells of the first church doing these two things in Acts 2:41-42.

[8]Vincent of Lerins, "Commonitorium," II, 3: *Quod semper, quod ubique, quod ab omnibus, creditum est.* See *Early Medieval Theology*, George E. McCracken and Allen Cabaniss, eds. (Philadelphia: The Westminster Press, 1957), 38.

CHAPTER 2

BELIEFS BAPTISTS SHARE WITH PROTESTANT CHRISTIANS

Baptists have sometimes debated whether or not they are Protestants. Half a century ago a popular version of their history was that Baptist churches, or at least proto-Baptist churches, existed throughout the history of the church. However, the consensus among historians today is that the Baptist movement was born among Puritans who separated from the Church of England very early in the seventeenth century. The first Baptist church was founded in 1608 or 1609 by English Separatists living in Holland. Given those historical origins, it is natural to ask what beliefs Baptists share with Protestants. There are five of these.

The Church Must Always Seek to Be Reformed

The New Testament presents the church as the body of Christ, as the bride of Christ, and as a holy nation.[1] The Roman Catholic Church has understood these and other New Testament images to mean that the church is indefectible. That is, while individual church members and leaders may and do make mistakes and commit sins, the church itself, as Christ's body, cannot sin or make mistakes. Some isolated factors in the church's life may be in error, but the direction of the church's faith and life cannot err because the church is Christ's body through which he lives and works in the world; it is his bride without spot or blemish.

This is a very reassuring doctrine, and it is understandable that the Roman Catholic Church came to believe it. Nevertheless, Martin Luther, John Calvin, Ulrich Zwingli, John Knox, and the other great Protestant reformers of the sixteenth century rejected it. What they saw around them led them to believe that the church was defectible rather than indefectible. They thought that the church not only could err but had erred, misleading people about the gospel of Christ. In place of the idea that the church is indefectible, the reformers presented another idea: *Ecclesia semper reformanda*, the church must constantly be reformed. Later theologians such as Paul Tillich have called this "the Protestant principle." It means that the church should never claim infallibility for itself but should always humbly seek to know God's will better and to be more devoted to God.

Baptists accept the Protestant principle. They do not believe that the church is indefectible. Instead, they speak consistently of the need of the church to be more committed to Christ and more faithful to his calling. The terms they use for this are "revival" and "renewal." Baptists are open to a revival of the life and commitment of God's people because they know that the church is imperfect. The church must never claim any kind of perfection for itself but must always seek humbly to be reformed in ways that bring it closer to God.

The Bible Alone Is the Written Word of God

As stated in chapter 1, all Christians believe that the Bible is the Word of God. This is as true of Roman Catholics as of Protestants. During the centuries when the Roman Catholic Church was the only church in the West, it came to believe in two sources of revelation: Scripture and tradition. That is, the official teaching of the church as given through councils and creeds, and interpreted by the magisterium or teaching authority of the bishops and popes, is the Word of God, just as the Bible is. The Protestant reformers rejected the claim that church tradition was a second source of revelation. Of course, they did not reject everything that had been said by councils and in creeds. For example, John Calvin's great book *The Institutes of the Christian Religion* included an extended commentary on the Apostles' Creed, which had been used in the Roman Catholic Church for more than a thousand years. What Protestants rejected was the claim that the authority of the church, the councils, the creeds, and the pope was on a par with the authority of the Bible. The Protestant position was summarized in the phrase, *sola Scriptura*, the Bible alone is the Word of God. Perhaps the most famous story about this from the Reformation era is about Martin Luther, who said at the Diet of Worms that he could never renounce the things he had written unless he were shown from Scripture that he was mistaken.

The Protestant emphasis on Scripture is a highly influential belief in Baptist life. Baptists love the Bible, and they take for granted its priority over all other written documents. In fact, Baptists find it unusual for any document other than the Bible to be studied in church, and when churches do study other documents, it is with the understanding that these are not authoritative in the way the Bible is. The preface to *The Baptist Faith and Message* says, "The sole authority for faith and practice among Baptists are the Scriptures of the Old and New Testaments."

Justification Is by Grace Alone through Faith Alone

Martin Luther learned from his study of the Bible that efforts to save oneself by prayers, good works, and so on, are not only doomed to fail but are in conflict with the Christian understanding of salvation as a free gift of God. The reformers retrieved the language of the apostle Paul: "We conclude that a person is put right with God only through faith, and not by doing what the Law commands" (Rom 3:28). Protestants call this principle *sola fide*, which means one is saved "by faith alone."

Baptists accept *sola fide*, and they emphasize it. In the nineteenth century, this principle led them to separate from some persons, who went on to form the Churches of Christ and the Disciples of Christ, over the question of whether or not baptism was essential to salvation. As important as baptism is to Baptists, they were persuaded that insisting that baptism is essential to salvation violates the principle of *sola fide*, and they refused to do that. When the reformers spoke of salvation, their preferred terminology was the legal idea of justification or acquittal before God; for Southern Baptists, the preferred terminology has come to be regeneration, the new birth into the family of God. Of course, both groups have used both terms. The new birth occurs when an individual responds to the gospel with repentance and faith. The fourth article of *The Baptist Faith and Message* says: "Repentance and faith are inseparable experiences of grace. Repentance is a genuine turning from sin toward God. Faith is the acceptance of Jesus Christ and commitment of the entire personality to Him as Lord and Saviour."

Southern Baptists sing many hymns that reflect their commitment to the principle of *sola fide*. "Only trust him, only trust him, / Only trust him now; / He will save you, he will save you / He will save you now."

They use phrases such as "coming home," "turn your eyes upon Jesus," and "I will arise and go to Jesus" to speak of putting one's faith in Jesus. Southern Baptists know quite well that this response to Christ results in salvation only because God is a God of grace. "Grace, grace, God's grace, / Grace that will pardon and cleanse within; / Grace, grace, God's grace, / Grace that is greater than all our sin."

All Believers Are Secure in Their Salvation

The Roman Catholic Church teaches that it is possible for Christians to forfeit their salvation either by egregious sin or by apostasy in belief. John Calvin and his successors denied that possibility. Southern Baptists share Calvin's conviction that those who are Christians will not forfeit their salvation. The fifth article of *The Baptist Faith and Message* emphasizes this:

> All true believers endure to the end. Those whom God has accepted in Christ, and sanctified by his Spirit, will never fall away from the state of grace, but shall persevere to the end. Believers may fall into sin through neglect and temptation, whereby they grieve the Spirit, impair their graces and comforts, bring reproach on the cause of Christ, and temporal judgments on themselves, yet they shall be kept by the power of God through faith unto salvation.[2]

The hymns that Baptists sing confirm this view. No hymn in *The Baptist Hymnal* speaks about the possibility of apostasy, and many confirm the security of God's children. "My faith has found a resting place not in device or creed; / I trust the ever living One, his wounds for me shall plead. / I need no other argument, I need no other plea, / It is enough that Jesus died, and that he died for me."

In one beloved hymn, God speaks these words to those with faith in Christ: "The soul that on Jesus hath leaned for repose / I will not, I will not desert to his foes; / That soul, though all hell should endeavor to shake, / I'll never, no, never, no, never forsake!"

All Believers Are Priests of God

The biblical message concerning priests is fascinating. The priests of the Old Testament era were an elite of male descendants of Levi and later of Aaron, but the Hebrew Scriptures contain two passages that prophesy a coming time when all of God's people will be priests

(Gen 19:5-6, Isa 61:5-6). The New Testament says that those prophecies are fulfilled in the Christian church. First Peter 2:4-10 is the most explicit text, and Christians are called priests in five passages in Revelation.

Prior to the Reformation of the sixteenth century, the Western church did not emphasize the priestly work of all Christians. Instead, priestly work was reserved for a male elite, the clergy of the church. For many conscientious Christians this became a sign of the oppression of the people by their leaders, and it was rejected by Martin Luther and the other reformers. Luther reaffirmed the priesthood of believers in his book *The Freedom of the Christian Man* and elsewhere. It was an idea whose time had come. In the New Testament, the priesthood of believers was a way of speaking of the privilege and the responsibility of all Christians to do things such as offer their lives as sacrifices to God and to do good works as sacrifices to God.[3] For Luther, however, the priesthood of all believers was a symbol not only for privilege and responsibility but also for freedom. Since the time of Luther many Christians have called upon the priesthood of believers in support of the proposals they have made concerning freedom of various kinds, especially religious liberty.

Understood as a symbol for Christian freedom, the priesthood of all believers is well represented in *The Baptist Faith and Message* (articles VI and XVII). Of the church that document says: "In such a congregation members are equally responsible," and of religious liberty it says: "A free church in a free state is the Christian ideal." It also says: "Baptists emphasize the soul's competency before God, freedom in religion, and the priesthood of the believer." The reference to "the soul's competency" calls for some explanation. The champion of that phrase was the most creative of Southern Baptist theologians, E. Y. Mullins. In a book titled *The Axioms of Religion: A New Interpretation of the Baptist Faith*, first published in 1908, Mullins defined "soul competency" as the freedom, ability, and responsibility of each person to respond to God for himself or herself. He argued that it is the most distinctive and important of Baptist beliefs, and that it is the "mother principle" from which six axioms may be derived. The theological axiom is that God has the right to be sovereign. The religious axiom is that all persons have a right of access to God. The ecclesiastical axiom is that all believers have a right to equal privileges in the church. The moral axiom is that only a free soul is a responsible soul. The religiocivic

axiom is a free church in a free state. The social axiom is, "You shall
love your neighbor as yourself." Mullins's use of the word "right" makes
it clear that he is speaking throughout of freedom. What the phrase
"priesthood of believers" affirms for Christians, Mullins's phrase "soul
competency" affirms for all human beings.

These, then, are five beliefs that Southern Baptists share with
Protestants but not with Roman Catholics: the church should always
be in the process of reformation; the Bible alone is the Word of God;
salvation is by God's grace through faith alone; all believers are secure
in their salvation; and all believers are priests before God. Interestingly,
the Roman Catholic Church seems to be having second thoughts
about some of these traditionally Protestant beliefs. The Second
Vatican Council, which met from 1962 until 1965, seems to have set
aside, or at least to have minimized, the two-source theory of revelation, and many Roman Catholics now speak quite freely of "the
priesthood of the faithful." Perhaps someday Baptists will hold these
beliefs in common with Roman Catholics as well as with Protestants.
In any case, these are part of the Southern Baptist theological heritage.

Notes

[1]Romans 12:3-8, Revelation 21:9, 1 Peter 2:9.

[2]Currently four phrases are in use among Southern Baptists for the issue with which
we are dealing here. They are "perseverance of the saints," "preservation of the saints,"
"the security of the believer," and "once saved, always saved." In using the word "secure,"
I am not opting for the superiority of that term to any of the others. For a criticism of some
of the phrases, see Dale Moody, The Word of Truth (Grand Rapids: William B. Eerdmans
Publishing Company, 1981), 361-62.

[3]See, for example, Romans 12:1 and Hebrews 13:15-16.

CHAPTER 3

BELIEFS UNIQUE TO BAPTISTS

Southern Baptists are part of a worldwide family of Baptists estimated to include about one hundred million people. Baptists share many things in common that, at least in the seventeenth century, were found almost exclusively among Baptists. In America today, however, some beliefs once distinctive to Baptists have come to be accepted by large numbers of people, including some who are not even church members.

The Baptist distinctives are what many people tend to associate especially with Baptists. That is understandable; these are important beliefs to Baptists. Throughout this book, however, we have been insisting that to understand Baptists one must attend not only to the beliefs distinctive to Baptists but also to the beliefs that Baptists hold in common with other Christian groups. The distinctively Baptist beliefs are all related to the two general ideas of church life and freedom. We shall describe them in terms of eight themes.

Only Believers Should Be Baptized

From its inception, the Christian church has practiced a rite of initiation that employs water and is called "baptism." Until the formation of the Society of Friends (Quakers) in the mid-seventh century, no church existed that did not practice baptism.[1] All of the churches agreed that baptism was an act of obedience to Christ and that it was to be done "in the name of the Father, and of the Son, and of the Holy Spirit" (Matt 28:19-20).

The first persons to be baptized were adults (Acts 2:37-41). It is unclear exactly when churches began to baptize infants. Doubtless it seemed a natural practice to people who were familiar with the Hebrew practice of circumcising male infants. We know that in the fourth century Augustine emphasized the theory that baptism eradicates original, inherited sin, and the widespread acceptance of this theory insured that the baptism of infants would continue. Across the centuries the vast majority of persons baptized have been infants born into Christian homes. Though believer's baptism was practiced first by Anabaptists, it was a dramatic moment in the history of the Christian church when a group of English women and men in Amsterdam, under the leadership of John Smyth, renounced the baptism which they had received as infants as no baptism at all, and submitted to baptism as adult believers. In the winter of 1608 or 1609 Smyth baptized first himself and then the members his congregation, thereby forming the first Baptist church.

Southern Baptists have retained the view that only believers should be baptized. They do not baptize infants, nor do they count their babies as members of the church. They do enroll them in Sunday school classes and other organizations, and they teach them the Bible and nurture them in the Christian faith, but children are not baptized until they are old enough to take a step of faith for themselves. This helps explain why so much of the preaching in Southern Baptist worship services is evangelistic; there are always non-church members present, even if only the children of the members.

In recent years Southern Baptists have tended to baptize more and more children at a very early age, sometimes as young as five years. However, this represents a revision of the understanding of the age at which it is possible for persons to come to faith on their own rather than a retreat from the principle of believers baptism.[2]

Given the distinctiveness of their belief about baptism, it is surprising to learn that Baptists do not sing very much about baptism. There are just three hymns about baptism in The Baptist Hymnal. Nor is much said about baptism in The Baptist Faith and Message, which simply states (VII): "Christian baptism is the immersion of a believer in water in the name of the Father, the Son, and the Holy Spirit." Commitment to believers baptism is so deeply imbedded and implicit in Baptist life and thought that it rarely needs to be made explicit. To the best of my knowledge, no Southern Baptist church has ever baptized an infant.

Believers baptism was originally a practice peculiar to the Baptists, but that is no longer the case. Other denominations such as the Disciples of Christ and the Assemblies of God also practice believers baptism. What was once a Baptist distinctive has become part of the heritage of a wider family of Christians.

Baptism Is by Immersion Only

Baptists have two beliefs about baptism that set them apart from most other Christians. One is that the only proper candidates for baptism are believers; the other is that the only proper mode of baptism is immersion. Baptists believe that baptism is proper only when it is biblical, and it is biblical only when believers are immersed.

All churches permit immersion as a mode of baptism; what is distinctive about Baptists is that, beginning about the middle of the seventeenth century, most Baptists disallowed any mode other than immersion. It is not certain when or why Christian churches first began to practice a mode other than immersion. Perhaps it was done very early, and perhaps the motivation was simply convenience. In any case, Baptists felt that to be true to the New Testament, the church must immerse believers fully, and that is what they did. By the 1640s immersion was the routine practice of the little Baptist churches in England, and it is the routine practice of Baptists today. Several other denominations have followed Baptists in this practice.

The Church Consists of Believers Only

Prior to the Reformation, everyone born in the West was baptized into the Roman Catholic Church, except those infants whose parents refused to allow them to be baptized, for example, parents who were Jews or, in Southern Spain, Muslims. Church and society were, for all practical purposes, the same people. But many sincere people came to long for something else. They longed to be a part of a community of faith in which all members were intentionally committed to Christ. The Reformation did not meet that need; the principle adopted at the Reformation was *cuius regio, eius religio*, that is, the official religion of a region would be the religion of the prince of that region. The government might grant greater or less tolerance to dissenters, but, except for the dissenters, the citizens of the nation were members of the church. Therefore the Reformation did not satisfy the desire many people felt to belong to an intentional faith community, a believers church.

The Puritans who separated from the Church of England were moving towards a believers church, but because they continued to baptize their children, their churches continued to comprise both intentional believers and those who were not yet intentionally committed to Christ. The Baptists took the next logical step when they restricted baptism to believers, thereby forming communities comprising only intentional believers. It was the fulfillment of the desire many people had felt for many years.

In the United States today, the idea of a believers church seems natural not only to Baptists but to many other Americans as well. Historian Martin Marty has written about the "baptistification" of American religion, by which he means the widespread acceptance among Americans of the idea that the only genuine religion is one that one accepts for oneself.[3] *The Baptist Faith and Message* (VI) defines a church as follows: "A New Testament church of the Lord Jesus Christ is a local body of baptized believers who are associated by covenant in the faith and fellowship of the gospel." The ideal of a believers church, like that of believers baptism by immersion, is assumed in Southern Baptist life more often than it is affirmed or defended. The Baptist conviction that churches should be intentional communities of faith is most evident in the Baptist practice of restricting baptism to those with faith in Christ.

Each Congregation Is Self-Governing

Once Baptists had established themselves in the seventeenth century as believers churches independent of the established Church of England, they faced the question of how they would be governed. The decision was made to follow the practice of their older cousins, the Congregationalists. Rather than looking to outsiders such as bishops or synods to make decisions concerning congregational life, each congregation was to govern itself. The debates about church government, also known as church order, are debates about how to find the will of God for a church. No Christians have defended the idea that churches are entitled to do whatever they, or their bishop or their synod, decide to do. The different forms of church government have always been presented as means for discerning the mind of Christ for the church.

Fundamentally there are three forms of church government.[4] One is *oligarchy*, which is government by a small, self-perpetuating group within the church; this form of government is practiced in the Roman Catholic Church. The second is *representative government*, which is government by a small, elected group within the church; this form is practiced in the Presbyterian churches. The third is *democratic government*, which is government by all of the members of the church; this form is practiced in Congregational and Baptist churches. Of course, all three forms get modified in practice. Nevertheless, these three forms of church government represent three different understandings of how the church may best discern the will of God for its common life.

All three have appealed to the New Testament for their justification. In some ways, Paul behaved like a bishop toward the churches to whom he wrote his letters; that historical example justifies the episcopal form of church government. Again, the first-century synagogues elected elders to govern the synagogue, and it is likely that some of the early churches did the same; that precedent justifies the Presbyterian form of government. Finally, Paul appealed to the church members at Corinth and elsewhere, rather than to their bishops or elders, to correct the problems in their common life; that call justifies the congregational form of government.

Today many scholars think that the churches of the New Testament era were governed in a variety of ways and that no writer of the New Testament intended to provide instructions about how the church should be governed. Many would agree with Eduard Schweizer: "There is no such thing as *the* New Testament church order."[5] It seems likely that this is true, which explains why it has been possible for the various forms of church government to have developed across the centuries.

When the first Baptists adopted the congregational form of church government, they followed the pattern of the Congregational churches. The pattern worked well, and it has been followed ever since. Southern Baptist congregations make decisions about all manner of things, confident that no person or group outside the congregation has any power over the congregation. The congregation may look outside for advice if it chooses to do so, but it is the church members themselves, not outsiders, who in the end make the decisions for the congregation. As might be expected, Southern Baptists do not sing about this idea. *The Baptist Faith and Message* (VI) says briefly: "This church is an autonomous body." In the seventeenth century autonomy was not self-evidently a good idea, but it has worked well for Baptists for almost four centuries. Today many other denominations have joined Baptists and Congregationalists in founding self-governing congregations.

All Members Share in the Church's Decision-Making

Once it is settled that local Baptist congregations are to be self-governing, one must deal with the issue of how each church makes decisions. The solution has been that they do it democratically. Each member participates equally in making decisions. Some people do not like to use the term "democratic" of Baptist congregations. They point out that, in a political democracy, voters are responsible to ask only what they want, whereas in Baptist churches, members are responsible to ask what they believe Christ wants. The distinction is a useful one, and it is reflected in *The Baptist Faith and Message* (VI), which says that a congregation operates "through democratic processes under the Lordship of Jesus Christ." To this it immediately adds: "In such a congregation members are equally responsible."

Whether or not the term "democratic" is used, the issue is clear. Granted that pastors and others exercise great authority and leadership in a congregation; granted that many decisions will be referred to committees and to other groups and individuals; granted that the ideal is to seek consensus rather than for a majority to abuse a minority in a church; still the question remains, "In the final analysis, who makes the decisions for the congregation?" And the Baptist answer is, "Under the Lordship of Jesus Christ, the people themselves make the decision by democratic procedures."

Congregations Should Cooperate with Each Other

Upon learning that each Baptist congregation is self-governing, one might assume that the congregations would have little or no relationship with each other. In principle, that is possible, but in practice, it is not the case. From the beginning, Baptist congregations have cooperated with each other; they have held conversations about doctrine and ethics, they have carried out ministries of education and benevolences together, and, especially among Southern Baptists, they have sponsored missionary work together. The cooperation of the congregations is never coerced, however; it is always voluntary. Among Southern Baptists, there are regional associations, state conventions, and the national organization called the Southern Baptist Convention, with which congregations may voluntarily associate themselves, but no one is to attempt to coerce any Baptist congregation to associate or to cooperate.

The primary motivation for cooperation among Southern Baptists is not so much theological as practical. It is not so much that the congregations believe in Christian unity in a way that requires them to cooperate, but rather that they know they cannot successfully carry out the work of missions effectively unless they cooperate. The founding document of the Southern Baptist Convention says that the Convention was organized to allow churches to do missions together; the Baptists who met in Augusta, Georgia, in 1845 to form the Southern Baptist Convention said that they were "organizing a plan for eliciting, combining, and directing the energies of the whole denomination in one sacred effort, for the propagation of the Gospel."[6] *The Baptist Faith and Message* (XIV) picks up some of the language of that founding document to affirm the appropriateness of cooperation among the congregations. In an article titled "Cooperation" we read:

> Christ's people should, as occasion requires, organize such associations and conventions as may best secure cooperation for the great objects of the Kingdom of God. Such organizations have no authority over one another or over the churches. They are voluntary and advisory bodies designed to elicit, combine, and direct the energies of our people in the most effective manner.

One great leader of Southern Baptists, Grady Cothen, has commented that on paper the Southern Baptist Convention will not work. That is a shrewd observation. Since cooperation among the 41,000 churches is entirely voluntarily, and since no person or group outside each congregation has any authority to compel the cooperation of the congregations, it is difficult to see, in principle, how the congregations could ever get anything done. Nevertheless, the Convention has been a very efficient organization. The reason is that Southern Baptists have trusted one another and felt loyalty to the Convention, and their trust and loyalty have led them to cooperate voluntarily and enthusiastically. They meet together, they share in common work, they own institutions such as the mission boards, they pray for one another, they accept members from each other's churches, and they bear one another's burdens. All of this is done voluntarily. It is facilitated by the great denominational service organizations such as the Woman's Missionary Union and LifeWay Christian Resources, but local congregations who draw upon the resources provided by these agencies do so voluntarily.

Occasionally one hears Southern Baptists complaining about the huge bureaucracy that has developed. This is quite understandable. Bureaucracy is a fact of modern life, and its problems are well-known.[7] Nevertheless, Baptists prefer bureaucrats to bishops because bureaucrats, unlike bishops, can be ignored with impunity.

Walter Shurden has commented that Southern Baptists have been one of the most "denominationalized" of church people. How did Southern Baptists ever develop so much loyalty to their denomination? Many factors contributed to this loyalty. Most of them have lived in the South. Many of them have attended Southern Baptist colleges and universities and participated in Southern Baptist summer camps. Many of their ministers have attended Southern Baptist seminaries. Southern Baptists have read books and Sunday school lessons by fellow Southern Baptists, and they contribute money to support Southern Baptist missionaries. The number of programs developed and conducted among Southern Baptists is so great that it is unlikely that any individual knows about all of them. For several decades the Convention has been so large that there has been little need for anyone to go outside it for much of anything; whatever one's gifts, they could be used within the Convention, and whatever one's interests, they could be developed within the Convention. The Convention became like a parallel universe to many Southern Baptists.

Southern Baptists sing about cooperation with each other: "Blest be the tie that binds our hearts in Christian love; / The fellowship of kindred minds is like to that above. / Before our Father's throne we pour our ardent prayers; / Our fears, our hopes, our aims are one, our comforts and our cares." The cooperation of Southern Baptists with each other has been encouraged in every way except one; it has never been coerced by any authority outside the local congregation.

Church and State Are to Be Separate

The relationship between church and state is an issue of freedom, just as the autonomy of local congregations and the making of congregational decisions by democratic means are issues of freedom. The Baptist record on church-state relations is consistent, and it begins with the earliest Baptists in England. The following summary of the Baptist heritage draws upon a wonderful brief pamphlet by the late William Estep.[8]

In 1611, a Baptist layman named Thomas Helwys led back to England part of the Baptist church formed in Amsterdam under the leadership of John Smyth. In 1612 he wrote a book titled *A Short Declaration of the Mystery of Iniquity*. He sent a copy to King James with a handwritten dedication in which he said: "The king is a mortal man, and not God, and therefore has no power over the immortal souls of his subjects, to make laws and ordinances for them, and to set spiritual lords over them. If the king have authority to make spiritual lords and laws, then he is an immortal God and not a mortal man."[9] For this audacious act Helwys was arrested and put in Newgate Prison, and he probably died there no later than 1616, a martyr for the cause of religious liberty. In 1614 another Baptist layman, Mark Leonard Busher, wrote *Religion's Peace: A Plea for Liberty of Conscience*, which he dedicated to King James and to Parliament. It is the first book published in the English language that is devoted entirely to the defense of religious liberty.

In America also, Baptists were early champions of religious liberty. Roger Williams was driven out of the Massachusetts Bay Colony by the Puritans there who claimed religious freedom for themselves but did not extend it to all others. In 1636 he founded what became the colony of Rhode Island, and in 1639 he founded at Providence the first Baptist church in the New World. He drew up a charter for Rhode Island that guaranteed religious liberty for all persons in the colony; the charter was granted in 1644. Williams once wrote: "All the Liberty of Conscience that ever I pleaded for, turns upon these two Hinges: that none of the Papists, Protestants, Jews, or Turks be forced to come to…Prayers or Worship; nor, secondly, compelled from their own particular Prayers or Worship, if they practice any."[10]

As the new nation was being founded a century and a half later, Baptists were working for assurances that it would be a nation with full religious freedom. The father of the Constitution was James Madison, an Anglican who had sympathies for the Baptists of Virginia. Madison learned from John Leland, a Baptist minister, that the Baptists were not happy with the proposed new Constitution because it did not specify that religious liberty would be given to all. Madison promised the Baptists that if they would help him work for ratification of the Constitution in Virginia, he would see to it that the first order of business of the new Congress would be to draw up amendments to the Constitution, forming a bill of rights for the people that included the right of religious liberty. Leland agreed, Virginia ratified the Constitution, and Madison kept his word; on June 8, 1789, he proposed the Bill of Rights to the new Congress. It was ratified by the states late in 1791.

The sixteen opening words of the First Amendment are the most influential words ever written in support of religious liberty: "Congress shall make no law respecting an establishment of religion, or prohibiting the free exercise thereof." This means that the government will be neutral toward religion, neither supporting it nor inhibiting it. Many interpretations have been offered of the First Amendment, and many arguments have been made concerning it, but the most important truth about it is that it has provided Americans with the greatest religious freedom ever enjoyed by any people in the history of the world. In a religiously pluralistic society, maximal religious liberty is possible only by means of a separation of church and state. The separation of church and state has worked. In America, the nation has flourished without an official religion to hold it together, and the church has flourished without the official support of the government.

Perhaps the success of this freedom in America has been made possible in part because the American people are a religious people. Although it is conventional to say that the American people are secular, the polls conducted by George Gallup and others make it clear that the United States is the most religious of the industrially developed nations by a considerable margin, with Ireland and Italy next and trailing far behind. One plausible suggestion for the continued religious commitment of the American people is that our religious faith provides us with moral values that in turn make possible the American way of life, including support for government neutrality toward religion. In any case, the point is that religious freedom has worked well in America, and Baptists have been champions of it.

Baptists do not sing about religious freedom very much, though *The Baptist Hymnal* does include "America the Beautiful," "My Country, 'Tis of Thee," and "The Star Spangled Banner." Baptists have affirmed religious liberty forcefully in *The Baptist Faith and Message* (XVII). The final article of that document is devoted to the topic, and it says in part: "God alone is Lord of the conscience, and He has left it free from the doctrines and commandments of men which are contrary to His Word or not contained in it. Church and state should be separate. The state owes to every church protection and full freedom in the pursuit of its spiritual ends."

Baptists have preached about religious liberty. Perhaps the most famous sermon ever preached by a Southern Baptist pastor was the one delivered by George W. Truett, the pastor of the First Baptist Church of Dallas, on the east steps of the Capitol in Washington on Sunday afternoon, May 16, 1920. Dr. Truett spoke of the historical effort of Baptists to secure religious freedom in the colonial period:

> On and on was the struggle waged by our Baptist fathers for religious liberty in Virginia, in the Carolinas, in Georgia, in Rhode Island and Massachusetts and Connecticut, and elsewhere, with one unyielding contention for unrestricted religious liberty for all men, and with never one wavering note. They dared to be odd, to stand alone, to refuse to conform, though it cost them suffering and even life itself. They dared to defy traditions and customs, and deliberately chose the way of non-conformity, even though in many a case it meant a cross. They pleaded and suffered, they offered their protests and remonstrances and memorials, and, thank God, mighty statesmen were won to their contention, Washington and Jefferson and Madison and Patrick Henry, and many others, until at last it was written into our country's Constitution that church and states must in this land be forever separate and free, that neither must ever trespass upon the distinctive functions of the other. It was preeminently a Baptist achievement.[11]

Americans who have lived all of their lives with religious liberty, with the understanding that religious faith is something one must accept for oneself, and with democracy in public life and in church life, sometimes find it difficult to appreciate the magnitude of the achievement of religious liberty in this country. But with a little historical imagination, one can perceive that what we now enjoy is a precious gift made possible by courageous, wise people who went before us, and that it is therefore to be appreciated, defended, and handed along to those who come after us.

Baptists Have No Creed but the Bible

Baptists make a technical distinction, one which is not made in all churches, between creeds and confessions.[12] Creeds and confessions often look very much alike; they deal with the same subjects and affirm the same things about those subjects. Nevertheless, the distinction between them is important to Baptists. The fundamental difference is that confessions are descriptive while creeds are prescriptive. Here is how William Lumpkin, the historian who has collected many of the Baptist confessions, expresses it:

> The Baptist Movement has traditionally been non-creedal in the sense that it has not erected authoritative confessions of faith as official bases of organization and tests of orthodoxy. An authority which could impose a confession upon individuals, churches, or larger bodies, has been lacking, and the desire to achieve uniformity has never been strong enough to secure adoption of a fixed creed even if the authority for imposing it had existed. Still, Baptists have recognized the valuable uses to which confessions of faith might be put.[13]

Confessions are descriptive statements, and Baptists have confessions. They describe the beliefs of the group or groups of Baptists who created or adopted them. They are written and adopted to help Baptists communicate their beliefs to their own children, to their fellow Baptists, to Christians in other denominations, and to persons who are not Christians. Baptists have been drawing up confessions ever since Baptist churches were first formed, very early in the seventeenth century.

The Southern Baptist Convention did not draw up a confession when it was organized in 1845, and for eighty years the Convention did not have an official, written confession. However, in the latter part of the nineteenth century, a Baptist confession called *The New Hampshire Confession*, which had been composed in 1833, became influential among many Baptists in the South. Then, in 1925, in response to a controversy concerning evolution, the Southern Baptist Convention adopted its first official confession; it was modeled on *The New Hampshire Confession*, and it was named *The Baptist Faith and Message*. In 1963, the Southern Baptists were engaged in another controversy, and one of the responses to it was the revision and adoption of the 1925 document; the 1963 statement was also titled *The Baptist Faith and Message*, and it is this statement to which we have referred throughout this book. Then, in 1998, the Convention added a brief section on the family to the 1963 statement, and in 2000 the Convention adopted a revision of the entire statement.

The first versions of *The Baptist Faith and Message* are to be understood as descriptions of the beliefs of the majority of Southern Baptists who met in conventions in Memphis in 1925 and in Kansas City in 1963. The preface to the 1963 version says this about confessions:

> They constitute a consensus of opinion of some Baptist body, large or small, for the general instruction and guidance of our own people and others concerning those articles of the Christian faith which are most surely held among us…. We do not regard them as complete statements of our faith, having any quality of finality or infallibility…. The sole authority for faith and practice among Baptists is the Scriptures of the Old and New Testaments. Confessions are only guides in interpretation, having no authority over the conscience.

The descriptive character of confessions is emphasized in this preface, and the preface also shows that the use of this confession or, for that matter, of any confession at all is entirely optional for Southern Baptists. Many Southern Baptist churches and church members have never even heard of *The Baptist Faith and Message*, and those who have heard of it are perfectly free to differ with it without thereby being disloyal to the Convention.

Baptists understand creeds to be entirely different from confessions. Creeds are authoritative statements of what one must believe in order to belong to a particular church. Baptists do not have creeds. They insist that the only written authority for Christian life and faith is the Bible. Their motto is: "No creed but the Bible." The preface to *The Baptist Faith and Message* describes Baptists as anti-creedal: "Such statements have never been regarded as complete, infallible statements of faith, nor as official creeds carrying mandatory authority."

Though the distinction between creeds and confessions may seem to be theoretical, in fact it has important practical implications. For example, in 1992 the president of the Foreign Mission Board of the Southern Baptist Convention, Keith Parks, resigned his position. He stated that he had philosophical differences with some of the members of the Foreign Mission Board. Specifically, he stated that he differed with them on the matter of creeds. Here is what he wrote:

> Our whole convention has moved more toward a creedal approach than a confessional approach with which I am comfortable. Although not a technical definition, my own understanding of the difference is that we as Baptists traditionally have made our confession of faith and said to others, "If you agree with this, let's cooperate and move together in a world mission effort." The creedal approach says, "This is what I believe, and I must examine your beliefs before I am sure that we can move together."[14]

In summary, Southern Baptists share eight beliefs with other Baptists around the world and with other Christians who have adopted Baptist beliefs. First, only believers should be baptized. Second, they should be baptized by immersion. Third, the result of believers baptism is a believers church. Fourth, each congregation should function autonomously. Fifth, each congregation should follow democratic procedures in its effort to discern God's will. Sixth, congregations should cooperate with each other in order to do their work better. Seventh, the Christian ideal is a free church in a free state, which means that government should be neutral toward religion and that church and state should be kept separate. Finally, Baptists have no creed but the Bible; they adopt descriptive confessions but not prescriptive creeds.

Notes

[1]Earlier in the church's history, some other groups had renounced baptism, but none of them has survived as a church.

[2]Knowledgeable writers employ three phrases for the baptism of believers: "believer's baptism," "believers' baptism," and "believers baptism." The same is true of a church of believers, which is called by informed writers "believer's church," "believers' church," and "believers church." I have chosen the third usage in each instance because I see no need for a possessive in either case.

[3]Martin E. Marty, "Baptistification Takes Over," *Christianity Today* (September 2, 1983), 33.

[4]Max Weber called forms such as these "ideal types." See Max Weber, *Essays in Sociology*, translated by H. H. Gerth and C. Wright Mills (New York: Oxford University Press, 1946), 323-24. Peter Berger says that the construction of ideal types is indispensable for understanding large and diverse fields of data; see Peter Berger, *The Heretical Imperative* (Garden City: Anchor Books, 1979), 60-61.

[5]Eduard Schweizer, *Church Order in the New Testament*, translated by Frank Clarke (London: SCM Press Ltd., 1961), 13.

[6]Quoted in Albert McClellan, *Meet Southern Baptists*, 29-30.

[7]See, for example, Peter Berger et al., *The Homeless Mind* (London: Penguin Books, 1973), Chapter 2.

[8]William R. Estep, Jr., "Religious Freedom" (Nashville: The Historical Commission of the Southern Baptist Convention, 1989).

[9]A photocopy of the dedication may be seen in Albert McClellan, *Meet Southern Baptists*, 12. I have provided modern spelling in the quotation.

[10]Quoted in Edwin S. Gausted, *Liberty of Conscience: Roger Williams in America* (Grand Rapids: William B. Eerdmans Publishing Company, 1991), 146.

[11]George W. Truett, "Baptists and Religious Liberty" (Nashville: The Sunday School Board of the Southern Baptist Convention, n. d.), 26.

[12]An alternative to the interpretation offered here is that the distinction between prescriptive creeds and descriptive confessions was not prominent until the twentieth century, and that earlier Baptists employed creeds prescriptively as long as they were voluntary and non-coercive, and especially, not sanctioned by the state. See Timothy George, "Conflict and Identity in the SBC" in *Beyond the Impasse? Scripture, Interpretation, and Theology in Baptist Life*, edited by Robison B. James and David S. Dockery (Nashville: Broadman Press, 1992), 202-207.

[13]William L. Lumpkin, *Baptist Confessions of Faith* (Philadelphia: Judson Press, 1959), 16.

[14]Letter from Helen Jean Parks and R. Keith Parks, to all foreign missionaries of the Southern Baptist Convention, March 27, 1992, 2.

CHAPTER 4

BELIEFS BAPTISTS SHARE
WITH REVIVALIST CHRISTIANS

The revivalist movement began more or less simultaneously in England and in the colonies of New England in the 1730s and 1740s. In England the great leaders were John Wesley, George Whitefield, and Charles Wesley, and in New England the great leader was Jonathan Edwards, though Whitefield made eight trips to the American colonies and made a notable contribution to the Great Awakening in the colonies.

The influence of this movement upon Christianity in America is immense, and the Southern Baptists have been affected by it as much as any group. The center of gravity for the theology of the Southern Baptists lies in the revivalist heritage. In fact, many Southern Baptists find it difficult to imagine a Christian church that does not accept the four beliefs discussed in this chapter.[1]

Every Individual Must Be Converted

All Christian churches hold out the possibility of conversion for persons who have no relationship to Christ or to the church. For example, the Roman Catholic Church would welcome the conversion of an atheist to Christian faith, and the Lutheran Church would welcome the conversion of an animist to Christian faith. Revivalism, however, takes this a step further and insists even those persons who have grown up in the church and have accepted what was taught them about Christian faith from their childhood must be converted in order to be genuine Christians.

This is difficult for many Christians to accept. They want to know what one is converted from if one grew up in Christian faith. They ask why it should be assumed that one's faith is not genuine unless one has arrived at it by means of a spiritual crisis. They point out that in the process of confirmation they internalized for themselves the faith that had been affirmed on their behalf when they were baptized as infants. They think of themselves as having come to faith before they were old enough to articulate it, and they are sure that it is no less real because they have had it since they were very young. They point out that many people feel loved by their parents long before they can articulate that, yet their conviction of their parents' love is no less real because they had it when they were so young. They also point out that many people who are genuinely in love did not come to that love through a personal crisis or by making a discrete decision, but their love is nevertheless real; similarly, many people who hold deeply to certain moral convictions did not arrive at them by a profound moral crisis, but their convictions are real nonetheless. It follows, they argue, that many people can have genuine faith in Christ without experiencing a profound spiritual crisis. It is, they say, possible for people who have grown up with Christian faith simply to intentionally affirm that for themselves; there is no need for them to be converted in the sense of trying to adopt that faith as though they did not already possess it.

That was not the view of the great revivalist leaders. As they looked out over Great Britain and the American colonies in the eighteenth century, they did not see, as others did, a Christian people who needed to be more obedient to God; rather they saw a people who were not Christians at all and who needed a conversion experience in order to become Christians. It is not enough, they argued, to be born into a Christian home in a Christian land and baptized into a Christian church. One must accept Christ for oneself; one must experience salvation personally. The revivalist movement transformed the Christian religion in England and in the colonies. No longer was the world divided into parishes and everyone regarded as a Christian and a member of an official church, except for those who intentionally opted out of the faith. Now every person, even those who were born and brought up in the most devout homes, had intentionally to commit her or his life to Christ in order to be a Christian and be a member of the churches.

In general, the churches that adopted the revivalist vision have flourished in America, and those that have rejected it have not. (The great exception is the Roman Catholic Church, which has grown by immigration and a high birth rate rather than by committing itself to revivalism). Southern Baptists adopted the revivalist vision. They emphasize the conversion experience. This is the center of gravity of their faith and life. For other Christians the center of gravity may be the Trinitarian understanding of God, or the principle of justification by grace through faith alone, or the Scriptures as the Word of God. Southern Baptists believe these things and think they are important, but the greatest emphasis in Southern Baptist life falls upon conversion. To this experience they return again and again in their thinking. Many of their church services are designed to foster this experience in people. For many Baptists the most important distinction among human beings is the distinction between those who have been converted and those who have not.

The Baptist Faith and Message (VI) displays both the assumption that conversion is necessary and the importance of the distinction between those who have and those who have not been converted. It says: "Salvation involves the redemption of the whole man, and is offered freely to all who accept Jesus Christ as Lord and Saviour."

Baptists sing about the experience of conversion in many popular songs and hymns. "Ye Must Be Born Again," they sing. Southern Baptist churches usually conclude their worship services with an invitation hymn that provides individuals with an opportunity to register decisions publicly. The decision may be to join the church, or to request prayer; but the decision most emphasized is the decision to be converted, to become a Christian. The hymn that is probably sung more frequently than any other during invitations is "Just As I Am," and it says: "Just as I am, without one plea / But that thy blood was shed for me, / And that thou bidd'st me come to thee, / O Lamb of God, I come! I come!" Another popular invitation hymn contains the question: "Why should we tarry when Jesus is pleading, pleading for you and for me? / Why should we linger and heed not his mercies, mercies for you and for me? / Come home, come home, ye who are weary come home; / Earnestly, tenderly, Jesus is calling, calling O sinner, come home!"

Occasionally one hears discussions among some Southern Baptists of the relationship between the conversion experience and Christian nurture. These discussions are important, but they do not diminish the importance of the conversion experience; they are rather attempts to see it as the most important moment in a process that began before conversion and continues after it.

The revivalist understanding of conversion did not originate among Baptists. It originated among Anglicans such as the Wesleys and Whitefield and among Congregationalists such as Jonathan Edwards. Nevertheless, in America the Southern Baptists are the principal beneficiaries of this view of conversion. One reason for this probably is the Baptist view of believers baptism. The Methodists, for example, continued to baptize their babies while preaching that all people need to be converted; understandably, for many Methodists the effect of the practice of baptizing infants gradually eclipsed the importance of the need for conversion. Baptists do not baptize their babies, so the message about conversion flourishes unhindered by their baptismal practice.

All Christians Should Be Sure of Their Salvation

The impression one gets in reading John Wesley's *Journal* is that nothing was more important to him than to gain an assurance that he truly was a child of God. In his own life he wrestled with this issue, as is well known, until he gained the assurance he sought in May 1738 at Aldersgate in London. Of that experience he wrote:

> In the evening, I went very unwillingly to a society in Aldersgate Street, where one was reading Luther's Preface to the Epistle to the Romans. About a quarter before nine, while he was describing the change which God works in the heart through faith in Christ, I felt my heart strangely warmed. I felt I did trust in Christ, Christ alone for my salvation; and an assurance was given me that he had taken away my sins, even mine, and saved me from the law of sin and death.[2]

The revivalist movement is not understandable apart from this concern for a personal assurance of salvation. In revivalist Christianity, it is not enough to have faith that Christ has died for the sins of the world, or even that Christ has died for one's own sins; one must also have faith that one has personally been forgiven and born anew into God's family. That was the message preached by John Wesley, and it is the message that Southern Baptists continue to preach today. Confidence that one has been saved is an indispensable component of the religious experience of Southern Baptists. It is an experience nurtured by the church in various ways. Individuals who feel assured of their salvation are encouraged to speak about their assurance, and those who lack assurance are encouraged to secure it.

Baptists wed this inner assurance of salvation to the outer security of their salvation that was discussed in chapter 2, and the result is a very powerful message: Christ has died for you; you can be saved; when you are saved, you can be assured that you are saved; and once you have been saved, God will protect you so that you will never lose your salvation.

There is a paradox about this message. It emphasizes two apparently contradictory beliefs. The free choice of an individual intentionally to trust Christ is paired with the belief that God will not permit the individual to forfeit salvation after he or she embraces it. But Baptists do not feel the paradox. What they feel is the most reassuring message possible: You are, and you always will be, a child of God. With such a reassuring message, it is not surprising that Southern Baptists have grown to become the largest non-Catholic body in America.

To people who do not share this heritage, the language of assurance seems to be presumptuous: Who is this, after all, who dares to claim certainty about his or her eternal destiny? While Southern Baptists are just as liable to become presumptuous as anyone else, the fact is that this tradition encourages people who are quite humble to speak confidently about the assurance they have of their salvation. In the revivalist tradition, even humble people learn to confess their confidence in God's mercy by saying, "I know that I will go to heaven when I die."

The Baptist Faith and Message (II) expresses assurance by speaking of the Holy Spirit: "His presence in the Christian is the assurance of God to bring the believer into the fullness of the stature of Christ." Baptists sing, "Blessed Assurance, Jesus Is Mine," and "I know whom I have believed / And am persuaded that he is able / To keep that which I've committed / Unto him against that day."

Evangelism Is the Primary Task of the Church

In chapter 1 we saw that all Christians believe that the Spirit guides the church on a worldwide mission. The revivalist belief about evangelism goes beyond that belief in two ways. First, in many churches the understanding of missions includes not only evangelism but worship, fellowship, education, and benevolences, whereas in revivalism the highest priority is always given to evangelism. Second, revivalist Christians believe that it is not enough to proclaim Christ; one must also attempt to persuade people to respond to Christ and, specifically, one must invite them to do so. Some Christians think that it is wrong to attempt to persuade people, but persuasion is an indispensable component of revivalism.

Southern Baptists are committed to the priority of evangelism, and they are committed to the need for persuasion in evangelism. They hold evangelistic campaigns, and they conduct workshops, conferences, and study programs on evangelism. They urge the work of evangelism on all churches and all individual Christians. They teach evangelism in their seminaries. We see this emphasis on evangelism in *The Baptist Faith and Message* (XI):

> It is the duty and privilege of every follower of Christ and of every church of the Lord Jesus Christ to endeavor to make disciples of all nations.... It is the duty of every child of God to seek constantly to win the lost to Christ by personal effort and by all other methods in harmony with the gospel of Christ.

The Baptist Hymnal also displays the emphasis on evangelism. In one hymn Baptists pray: "Lord, speak to me, that I may speak in living echoes of thy tone; / As thou has sought, so let me seek thy erring children lost and lone." They also pray: "Lord, lay some soul upon my heart, and love that soul through me; / And may I bravely do my part to win that soul for thee." The emphasis on evangelism is clear in a song by Fanny Crosby: "Rescue the perishing, care for the dying, snatch them in pity from sin and the grave; / Weep o'er the erring one, lift up the fallen, tell them of Jesus the mighty to save."

Missions Is a Priority for the Church

The modern missionary movement is usually said to have begun in the 1790s. One of the pioneers in that movement was William Carey, an English cobbler and Baptist minister who gave his life in missionary service in India. The modern missionary movement is a direct product of the revivalist movement, and the emphasis on missions is a direct product of the emphasis on evangelism associated with revivalism. It is not that missions was restricted to evangelism; in fact, church leaders quickly learned that missionary work succeeds best when it includes works of compassion and education as well as direct evangelism. But it is clear that evangelism was a major goal of the modern missionary movement, and for that reason we here associate the two.

Across the years, the best way to catch a sense of the heartbeat of Southern Baptists has been to attend a presentation of the Foreign Mission Board (now International Mission Board) on the Wednesday evening when the Convention meets in June of each year. The Convention has been faithful to the purpose of those who organized the Board to be "a plan for eliciting, combining, and directing the energies of the whole denomination in one sacred effort, for the propagation of the Gospel."[3] It is not an exaggeration to say that the Convention has no sufficient reason to exist apart from missions.

The Baptist Faith and Message does not contain separate articles on evangelism and missions but a single article titled "Evangelism and Missions." In *The Baptist Hymnal*, there are not two groups of hymns, one on missions and one on evangelism, but one group titled "Evangelism and Missions." The missionary aspect is quite clear in many of the hymns. For example: "There's a call comes ringing o'er the restless wave, 'Send the light! Send the light!' / There are souls to rescue, there are souls to save, Send the light! Send the light! / Send the Light! The blessed gospel light; / Let it shine from shore to shore!" Baptists admonish one another: "We have heard the joyful sound: Jesus saves! Jesus saves! / Spread the tidings all around: Jesus saves! Jesus saves! / Bear the news to every land, climb the steeps and cross the waves; / Onward! 'tis our Lord's command; Jesus saves! Jesus saves!" And they sing unselfconsciously: "We've a story to tell to the nations, that shall turn their hearts to the right." They encourage one another with these words: "O Zion haste, thy mission, high fulfilling, to tell to all the world that God is Light; / That he who made all nations is not willing one soul should perish, lost in shades of night. / Publish glad tidings, tidings of peace, tidings of Jesus, redemption and release."

In summary, Southern Baptists share four beliefs with others who have embraced the great movement of revivalism that began in England and the American colonies in the eighteenth century. First, they believe that every individual must be converted to faith in Christ; growing up in a Christian home or church is no substitute for a personal experience of conversion. Second, all converts can and should have a deep personal assurance that they are saved. Third, evangelism is the most important work of the church. Finally, God calls the church to be a missionary people and to evangelize the world.

Notes

[1]Two Southern Baptist historian/theologians, James Leo Garrett and E. Glenn Hinson, have debated whether it is proper to call Southern Baptists "evangelicals," a question that is relevant to the present chapter because what I am calling "revivalism" is often referred to as "the evangelical revival." In my judgment, it is right to say that Southern Baptists are evangelicals inasmuch as they have been influenced by the revivalist movement and share many things in common with the wider evangelical movement in America today, things such as a vigorous commitment to evangelism. On the other hand, it is right to say that Baptists are not evangelicals inasmuch as they existed prior to the revivalist movement and they have distinctive beliefs and practices such as believers baptism that are not shared by all members of the evangelical movement in America. See James Leo Garrett, E. Glenn Hinson, and James E. Tull, Are Southern Baptists "Evangelicals"? (Macon GA: Mercer University Press, 1983). For an illustration of the fact that the revivalist tradition is the center of gravity for many Southern Baptists, notice that the first chapter of a fine book by William Tuck emphasizes religious experience and evangelism and links these to believers baptism and a believers church. See Our Baptist Tradition, William Powell Tuck (Macon GA: Smyth & Helwys Publishing, Inc., 1993), chapter 1.

[2]John Wesley, journal entry for May 15, 1738. See Albert C. Outler, ed., John Wesley (New York: Oxford University Press, 1964), 66.

[3]Quoted in Albert McClellan, Meet Southern Baptists, 29-30.

PART TWO

THE
MINORITY
TRADITIONS

CHAPTER 5

ANABAPTIST BELIEFS

Now we shall examine six clusters of beliefs that have been available to Southern Baptists, which significant minorities of Southern Baptists have accepted, but which before 1979 had not become part of the majority tradition of Southern Baptists. The first minority tradition is that associated with the Anabaptists, the radical reformers of the sixteenth century. The word *Anabaptist* is used of many different groups in the sixteenth century. Some of them, such as the unitarian Socinians, have had little influence on modern Baptist life. Others have definitely contributed certain ideas to modern Baptist life. We shall consider three of those ideas.

True Christians Are a Sect Opposed to Society

The German scholar Ernst Troelsch once distinguished between two types of Christian groups, which he called the *church-type* and the *sect-type*.[1] By church-type he meant groups of Christians who are more or less at home in their society, who accept many things about their culture, and who contribute to and may even exercise hegemony over the society and culture of which they are a part. They are inspired by biblical passages that tell the people of Israel to inherit the promised land. The sect-type are groups of Christians who are not at home in their society but are alienated from it. They resist their culture at almost every point. They make no effort to contribute to their society and culture or to influence them, but only attempt to escape their influence as much as possible. They are inspired by the biblical passages that tell the church not to love the world or the things in the world.

Baptists began as a sect-type group. In England in the seventeenth century their ideas about baptism and about religious liberty were radical, and they were often persecuted for these ideas. The first Baptists in the American colonies continued to function as a sect-type group. However, when Baptists in America accepted the revivalist movement, things began to change. Baptists became a large group in America, and in a democratic nation, a large group is a powerful group. One recent book title expressed it vividly: *In the South the Baptists Are the Center of Gravity*.[2] Baptists evolved from a sect-type to a church-type in the South. This does not mean that Southern Baptists accept everything in their society and culture. In many ways, they feel that their culture has become less Christian than it once was. Baptists have opposed things such as alcoholic beverages, casino gambling, and abortion. But they oppose these things not as an insignificant minority, but as a large and influential group with good reasons for thinking that they are entitled to influence society.

Among Southern Baptists in the twentieth and twenty-first centuries there have been individuals who wanted Southern Baptists to return to the sect-type group they once were. These people have worried that the religion of Southern Baptists has become too much a religion of the nation, a civil religion, rather than a personal, intentional commitment to follow Jesus Christ as his faithful disciples. For example, they are distressed by the fact that Southern Baptists conformed to Southern white society by accepting slavery in the nineteenth century and racial segregation in the twentieth, and they call Southern Baptists to return to a sect-type mentality that will enable them to resist the values of the larger society more successfully.

Southern Baptists have changed their attitudes toward race, but they have not become a sect-type group in order to do so. They began to change their attitude toward slavery when the South lost the Civil War, and they began to change their attitude toward segregation when the government of the United States made segregation in public life illegal. Even now many Southern Baptist churches probably would not welcome black members with enthusiasm, which is ironic, given the deep commitment Southern Baptists have to missions. This irony has sometimes been displayed when black young people converted in Southern Baptist missionary work abroad have been denied membership in local Southern Baptist churches in the United States when they came here to attend college.[3]

All is not gloomy, of course. Many Baptist churches do welcome black members, and the North American Mission Board of the

Southern Baptist Convention (formerly the Home Mission Board) is working closely with predominantly black churches. Yet it cannot be said that the Southern Baptists have managed to oppose the segregationist values of Southern white society as successfully as a sect-type group might have done.

Christians Should Never Go to War

Across the centuries, Christians have held three different views about war. Some Christians believe in holy war; that is, they feel that God calls people today, just as God called Israel long ago, to go to war, and war is an activity that is God's will and is blessed by God. That was the attitude taken by many Christians during the Crusades of the Middle Ages.

Most Christians hold a second view known as "just war." The idea is that war is an evil rather than a good, but sometimes it is the lesser of two evils available to us; not to go to war would be even worse. Just war theory has two parts. Certain criteria have been developed for determining when it is just to go to war (*jus ad bellum*), and other criteria have been developed for determining whether a war is being conducted in a just manner (*jus in bello*). Examples of criteria for justly going to war are that the enemy has committed or threatened aggression, that every effort has been made to deal with the aggression short of war, that war has been officially declared, that there is a reasonable hope of victory, and that the gains of stopping the aggression will outweigh the suffering the war will cause. Examples of criteria for justly conducting a war are that no actions be taken against non-combatants and that excessive force not be used. The majority of Christians have accepted the thesis that war is sometimes a regrettable necessity.

The third view of war is that it is never the will of God for Christians to go to war or to use violence against others. The great inspiration for this view is, of course, the life and teachings of Jesus. He taught his followers not to return evil for evil but to turn the other cheek. Many Christians, including many Anabaptists in the sixteenth century, have believed that loyalty to Christ requires that we be pacifists.

Most Southern Baptists accept just war theory. World War II is the example to which many refer when they talk about war. Was it not better, they ask, to resist Hitler and Naziism by means of war than to have abdicated our responsibility toward our European allies? However, some Southern Baptists have called upon the Convention to adopt the pacifist position. A paper called *Baptist Peacemaker* and an organization called The Baptist Peace Fellowship of North America, while not exclusively pacifist, have led many Southern Baptists to think about this issue. The message of pacifism is attractive to Southern Baptists, not least because it appeals so directly to the teachings of Jesus, but the majority of Southern Baptists have not become pacifists.

Christians Should Share Their Possessions Communally

Across the centuries Christians have experimented with various forms of communal life, inspired by texts such as Acts 2:44-45: "All the believers continued together in close fellowship and shared their belongings with one another. They would sell their property and possessions, and distribute the money among all, according to what each one needed." The most famous examples of communal living are the convents and monasteries found in the Eastern churches and in the Roman Catholic Church, but many efforts at communal living have been made by Protestants. Some Anabaptists practiced communal living, and in America in the nineteenth century numerous communities were formed that held their possessions in common. Most Southern Baptists have not been open to suggestions that they share their possessions communally. However, one influential Southern Baptist minister, Clarence Jordan, did establish a successful experiment in communal living, Koinonia Farm near Americus, Georgia, from which has come the very prominant movement known today as Habitat for Humanity.

One of the justifications for communal life is that justice requires that everyone share equally in wealth. In fact, two different understandings of justice are found in public conversations about the subject. One says that it is fair and just for people to benefit from what they have grown, earned, invented, discovered, or inherited; it is unjust to deprive them of what is theirs. The other view says that it is fair and just for all Americans to have food, clothing, housing, a good education, and meaningful work. The problem, of course, is that these two understandings of justice are incompatible. The only way to insure that all Americans have food is to take away some of what some people have earned and give it to those who either cannot or do not successfully manage to earn enough to buy the food they need. It is not possible to have both of these kinds of justice in the world, because achieving one of them insures that the other will not be achieved.

The first understanding of justice receives support from biblical passages such as "If a man will not work, he shall not eat" (2 Thess 3:10). The second understanding of justice receives support from the prophets of Israel such as Amos who condemn the powerful people in Israel not only for stealing from the poor but for the fact that there are poor people in Israel at all. Most Americans feel the call to the first form of justice more deeply than the call to the second, and the collapse of the governments of the former Soviet Union and of Eastern Europe suggests that many people in the world today agree. The second sense of justice gives rise to the formation of communes. The attractions of communal living are great, as attested by the continuing success of monasteries in the Roman Catholic Church, but among Southern Baptists the call to communal sharing is decidedly a minority tradition.

The Anabaptist tradition still exercises an influence upon the Christian church generally and upon Southern Baptists in particular, especially in matters of peace and justice and the need to resist the values of the society and culture within which the church lives. But among Southern Baptists it remains a decidedly minority tradition.

Notes

[1]Ernst Troelsch, *The Social Teaching of the Christian Churches*, translated by Olive Wyon (New York: Macmillan Publishing Company, 1931), I, 331ff.

[2]Edward L. Queen, *In the South the Baptists Are the Center of Gravity: Southern Baptists and Social Change, 1930–1980* (Brooklyn: Carlson Publishing Inc, 1991).

[3]Will D. Campbell, *The Stem of Jesse: The Costs of Community at a 1960s Southern School* (Macon GA: Mercer University Press, 1995).

CHAPTER 6

CALVINISTIC BELIEFS

The first Baptists were English citizens who lived in the Netherlands when that country was engaged in a prolonged public debate about Calvinism. In 1618–1619 the leaders of the Dutch church held a synod in the city of Dort (today, Dordrecht) in which they adopted five articles that have become a normative way of expressing the distinctive teachings of Calvinism. Since they were living in the Netherlands, the first Baptists were aware of the debate about Calvinism, and in a series of confessions they made it clear that they were opposed to the Calvinism that finally was adopted by the Dutch church.

The five Canons of Dort may be presented in English by the use of the acronym TULIP, which refers to *total depravity, unconditional election, limited atonement, irresistible grace,* and the *perseverance of the saints.*[1] This is a convenient device, but, in fact, the sequence of the five articles at Dort was different. The first article concerned predestination; the second concerned limited atonement; the third concerned total depravity; the fourth and fifth were as above. The actual acronym from Dort was therefore ULTIP.

All five of these Calvinistic beliefs are related to salvation. Southern Baptists agree with Calvinists that salvation is a very important issue, and, as we have seen, they continue to believe in the final perseverance of the saints, as Calvinists do. This is the only one of the five themes of Dort that is part of the beliefs of the majority of Southern Baptists.[2] The other four themes are held by an articulate minority of Southern Baptists. Some of them teach in colleges and seminaries, and some have organized a group called Founders Ministries; the name reflects the fact that many of the founders of the

Southern Baptist Convention were devoted Calvinists. Founders Ministries publishes a journal called *The Founders Journal*.

Calvinism is an enormously attractive theological system. It has good claims to be true to Scripture, and it is conducive to personal humility, to corporate worship, and to sophisticated theological reflection. It is sometimes accused of being antithetical to evangelism and missions, and that is an understandable accusation, but the Calvinists among Southern Baptists today are highly committed to missions and evangelism. Great evangelists such as George Whitefield and Jonathan Edwards were Calvinists; on the other hand, the great evangelist John Wesley intentionally rejected Calvinism. Our purpose here is to describe the four themes of Calvinism held by an articulate minority of Southern Baptists, and we shall follow the sequence that was followed at Dort.

God Unconditionally Elects Some People to Be Saved

The Bible has a great deal to say about election and predestination. Calvinists have studied these words closely and have concluded that God has predestinated some individuals to be saved and others to be damned. They insist that God did not first foreknow how people would respond to God and then predestinate them; rather, God first predestinated how people would respond to God and then foreknew that they would so respond. The usual name for this is "double predestination."[3] Those who are predestined to be saved are the elect; those who are predestined to be damned are the reprobate.

This is not a view held by most Southern Baptists. They believe that God chooses to save those who choose to put their faith in Christ. Baptists are open to the idea that God has foreknowledge of which individuals will put their faith in Christ, but they do not believe that God in his sovereignty predestines to save some and to damn others. They believe that God wants all people to be saved but that God will not override their freedom in order to save them. If people make a decision to accept Christ, God saves them; if they make a decision to reject Christ, God sadly allows them to remain unsaved.

Most Southern Baptists are uneasy with the Calvinistic understanding of double predestination. To them it seems to be arbitrary and contrary to God's love for all people. They do not know how to reconcile double predestination with their convictions that "God so loved the world" (John 3:16) that God "will have all men to be saved, and to come unto the knowledge of the truth" (1 Tim 2:4). They are aware that some biblical texts sound very much like double predestination, such as "Jacob have I loved, but Esau have I hated" (Rom 9:13), but they read these texts in light of other texts such as "the Lord is not…willing that any should perish, but that all should come to repentance" (2 Pet 3:9). Southern Baptists are uneasy with double predestination for another reason. As we have seen, they emphasize evangelism and missions. Their belief in evangelism and missions is supported by certain other beliefs. One of these is that God loves everyone in the world. A second is that God wants everyone to be saved. A third is that every person who hears the gospel can put his or her trust in Christ and be saved. A fourth is that Christians make it possible for people to be saved by preaching the gospel to them. These ideas are the engine that drives missionary and evangelistic work of the Southern Baptists. Southern Baptists resist double predestination because it undermines the motives that compel them to do missionary and evangelistic work.

As we saw earlier, Calvinism does not have to undermine evangelism and missions; there have been and are Calvinists who are committed to these things. But Southern Baptists suspect that they would lose their commitment to these things if they adopted Calvinism, and there is good reason to think they are right about that.

Christ Died for the Elect Only

The New Testament presents the meaning of the death of Christ in many ways. For example, it is presented as a sacrifice that takes away sins, as a victory over the devil, as a revelation of the love of God, and as an example that Christians are to imitate.[4] All of these understandings of the death of Christ may be found in the writings of John Calvin. Along with them, Calvin presented an understanding of the atonement that became the most important one for many of his successors. Drawing upon Isaiah 53 and other biblical passages, he argued that Christ died as a substitute for sinners and experienced God's punishment for human sins. The name for this understanding of the death of Christ is "penal substitution," "penal" because Christ was experiencing the penalty for sin and "substitution" because Christ was the substitute for sinners.

The penal substitutionary understanding of Christ's atoning work may be interpreted quantitatively. That is, it is quite reasonable to ask of this understanding, "Did Christ suffer the penalty for the sins of all people, or only the penalty for the people who are going to be saved?" The Calvinist answer is that Christ paid the penalty for the sins of the elect only, not for the sins of the entire world. This view is called "limited atonement" because it says that God intended the atonement to be for the sins of a limited group, and not for the sins of the entire world. The view that Christ died for the sins of all the world is called "general atonement." Both views seem to have support in the New Testament. For example, Paul said that "Christ died for *our* sins" (1 Cor 15:3), which can be understood as a reference to a limited atonement. And John wrote that Christ "is the propitiation for our sins: and not for ours only, but also for the sins of the whole world" (1 John 2:2), which supports a general atonement. Limited atonement fits very neatly, of course, with double predestination; there would seem to be no point in Christ dying for the sins of persons whom God has predestinated to be damned.

Many Southern Baptists accept the penal substitutionary understanding of atonement, but most of them think that Christ died for the sins of all the world. Only a minority of them think that Christ died just for the elect.

All People Are Totally Depraved

In chapter 1 we observed that all Christians believe that the world is a fallen world and that all human beings are sinners. Calvinism takes this belief a step further. It says that all people are depraved. The Bible can be called upon in support of this view. In Romans 7 Paul speaks of human beings as enslaved by sin, and in Ephesians 2 he speaks of people as dead in their sins; these texts certainly sound like descriptions of total depravity.

How are we to understand Paul's language about slavery and death? Calvinists understand these teachings to mean two things. First, human beings cannot save themselves; if they are to be saved, it must be God who saves. Second, until they have been born again, human beings are unable to respond to God; since they are spiritually dead, they cannot repent or have faith in God or pray.

All Christians, including Southern Baptists, agree with the first interpretation of slavery and death. Human beings cannot save themselves. They are dependent upon God for their salvation. However, most Southern Baptists do not agree with the second interpretation.

They think that the texts about being enslaved to sin and dead in sin mean that we are unable to save ourselves, but they do not think they also mean that we cannot repent and have faith in Christ when the gospel is preached to us. "Whosoever will may come," Baptists sing, urging people to come to Christ for salvation.

Calvinists defend their belief that spiritually dead people cannot respond to God by saying that, if human beings were able to repent and to have faith, they would be contributing to their salvation. But the majority of Southern Baptists do not agree. They believe that salvation is entirely a work of God done by God's grace, which is freely and generously given to undeserving human beings. Faith and repentance are responses made by persons who are still enslaved and dead in their sins, by which they receive salvation and new life that God has provided through Jesus Christ. Repentance and faith do not contribute to salvation; they are the way one who is enslaved by sin receives the salvation from sin that God has provided.

God's Grace Is Finally Irresistible

Calvinists believe that God's grace cannot finally be resisted by those sinners whom God has predestined for salvation. This belief is closely tied to the earlier ones. If God has predestined that certain persons will be saved, then God's actions in their lives to awaken them to faith and repentance must inevitably result in their coming to faith and so to salvation. Calvinists believe that God acts with a grace that in some mysterious way is finally irresistible. Of course, God does this toward the elect only, not toward others, the non-elect. Calvinists believe that a theology that does not affirm the final irresistibility of God's grace effectively forfeits the sovereignty of God. They ask, "If sinners — who are dead in their sins at that — can finally resist God, then who exactly is in charge of the world?"

Most Southern Baptists do not believe in the final irresistibility of God's grace. They believe that people can and do finally resist God's grace and that their resistance results in their never being saved. But this does not mean that Southern Baptists do not believe in God's sovereignty. They believe that God is very much in charge of the world, but they believe that God has chosen to give human beings the power to make decisions, which God then respects. They believe that for God to give such freedom and then to respect it does not constitute a diminishment of the sovereignty of God but a recognition of the way in which the sovereign God has chosen to relate to human beings.

In conclusion, what remains of the TULIP of Calvinism among the majority of Southern Baptists is the final belief that all the saints persevere to the end. The majority of Southern Baptists do not accept double predestination, limited atonement, depravity understood as inability to respond to the gospel, and the irresistibility of God's grace.

When the Southern Baptist Convention was formed in 1845 Baptist theologians such as James P. Boyce and John L. Dagg were more committed to the theological system of Calvinism than most Southern Baptists are today. "Any casual observer of the contemporary Southern Baptist scene can readily observe that the Doctrines of Grace no longer hold sway over the majority of Southern Baptist people, or even a significantly large minority of them."[5] In this sense the Southern Baptists who believe in Calvinism might seem to be entitled to think that they are conservatives attempting to retrieve a tradition once held by many Southern Baptists. But there is a complicating factor. Historian Walter Shurden has pointed out that when the Convention was organized in 1845 it already comprised four traditions.[6] The Convention includes what Shurden called the Charleston tradition, which was Calvinistic. It also included a Sandy Creek tradition, which minimized Calvinism and emphasized evangelism. It also included a Georgia tradition, which represented the Southernness and regionalness of the Convention, and a Tennessee tradition, which emphasized the distinctiveness of Baptist churches. To these four the late John Loftis has added a fifth, an evangelical-denominational tradition, which is strong in the Southwest.[7]

The point here is that, while there were among the founders of the Convention men who were fully committed to Calvinism, from the beginning there were others in the Convention for whom the center of gravity was not to be found here but rather in the commitment of the Convention to evangelism. To put it differently, evangelism, with its presuppositions and implications, was a commitment that was sufficient for the formation and operation of the Convention for some Baptists but not for others. Since the Convention was a hybrid from its inception, it is possible to speak of the widespread lack of commitment to most of the Calvinistic beliefs today not as a defection, but as the triumph of one of the early traditions over another. For more than a century the Sandy Creek tradition has won the hearts of more Southern Baptists than the Charleston tradition. This means, then, that the Southern Baptists who resist Calvinism may be called traditional Baptists in the sense that the first Baptists resisted Calvinism, and in the sense that today most Southern Baptists resist it.

Notes

[1]See Philip Schaff, The Creeds of Christendom. III, The Evangelical Protestant Creeds, fourth edition (New York: Harper and Brothers, 1919), 550-97.

[2]For the case that Baptists are more closely aligned with the magisterial Reformation than is suggested here, see Timothy George, "The Reformation Roots of the Baptist Tradition" in Review and Expositor (Winter, 1989), 9-22.

[3]A milder version of this is single predestination, which says that God predestinated some people to be saved and did not so predestinate others. The end result of the two views is the same.

[4]See Hebrews 9:1-14, Colossians 2:15, 1 John 4:9, and 1 Peter 2:21, respectively.

[5]Thomas J. Nettles, By His Grace and For His Glory: A Historical, Theological, and Practical Study of the Doctrines of Grace in Baptist Life (Grand Rapids: Baker Book House, 1986), 244. For a history of this change see the chapter on predestination in Paul A. Basden, ed., Has Our Theology Changed? (Nashville: Broadman & Holman, 1994).

[6]Walter Shurden, "The 1980–81 Carver-Barnes Lectures" (Wake Forest: Southeastern Baptist Theological Seminary, 1980).

[7]John Loftis, Factors in Southern Baptist Identity as Reflected by Ministerial Role Models, 1750–1925 (Unpublished doctoral dissertation, Southern Baptist Theological Seminary, 1987).

CHAPTER 7

LANDMARK BAPTIST BELIEFS

The Landmark Baptist movement originated in the Northern United States early in the nineteenth century. In the South the prominent leaders of the movement were J. R. Graves, J. M. Pendleton, and A. C. Dayton. By the late nineteenth century they had managed to make Landmark concerns the most discussed issues in Southern Baptist life. Those issues were essentially issues of ecclesiology. The movement took its name from Proverbs 22:28: "Remove not the ancient landmark, which thy fathers have set." The Landmark leaders did not feel that they were originators of a new movement but rather that they were strict, old-fashioned Baptists who were setting up landmarks that had been allowed to crumble. The summary of Landmark concerns will be presented as two themes.

Baptists Should Separate from Non-Baptists

We have seen that Baptists hold two distinctive ideas about baptism, namely, that it should be by immersion and that only believers should be baptized. The result is a believers church. The Landmark Baptists took this idea a step further. They reasoned that, if the New Testament teaches that a believers church is the only genuine church, it follows that Methodist and Presbyterian churches are not really churches at all but religious societies. The Landmark Baptists reserved the word "church" for Baptist churches exclusively.

The Landmark attitude toward a believers church differs from the original attitude Baptists had toward a believers church. The original attitude was that a believers church was a dream for which many people longed, and then, in the seventeenth century, it became a dream come true, a privilege to be enjoyed, and a blessing from God. The

Landmark Baptist emphasis was different. They understood a believers church as the creation of a people who had been faithful to God's Word when other people were unfaithful; it was the achievement of real Bible believers, with the help of God no doubt, but their achievement all the same. The Landmark attitude toward those such as Methodists and Presbyterians who did not have a believers church was not one of sadness that they were missing a blessing, but one of hostility and opposition because they were not being faithful to the New Testament.

The Landmark Baptists were prepared to follow the argument wherever it led, and it led them to believe that Baptists should separate from non-Baptists because of the latter's unfaithfulness to the New Testament. So, for example, J. M. Pendleton wrote a tract titled "Ought Baptists to invite pedobaptists to preach in their pulpits?" (a "pedobaptist" is one who baptizes babies), and he answered his own question with a vigorous "No." J. R. Graves published the tract under the title, "An Old Landmark Reset."

One of the arguments by which the Landmark Baptists defended their views was historical. They believed that there had always been a faithful group in the world. Their historians saw the history of dissent in the church — the Montanists, the Donatists, the Waldenses, the various Anabaptist groups, and so on — as constituting an unbroken chain of believers churches across the centuries. Just as Roman Catholics believed in apostolic succession, the claim that there was in the Roman church an unbroken chain of ordinations of priests and consecrations of bishops reaching back to the apostle Peter, so the Landmark Baptists affirmed a "trail of blood," that is, that there was an unbroken chain of believers churches reaching back to the churches of the New Testament era. In effect, the trail of blood meant that there was a succession of Baptist churches, though with other names, across the centuries. This view is not held by many historians today. It supported the Landmark polemic against non-Baptists, but the historical sources do not support it.[1]

It is clear that the Landmark belief that Baptists should separate from non-Baptists has influenced the Southern Baptist Convention. For example, the Southern Baptist Convention almost never enters into cooperative arrangements with non-Baptist groups. When the ecumenical movement was born early in the twentieth century, Southern Baptists took the lead in forming a new organization, the

Baptist World Alliance, as an alternative to participation in organizations such as the National Council of Churches and the World Council of Churches which include non-Baptists.

Nevertheless, most Southern Baptists have not accepted the Landmark invitation to separate completely from non-Baptists or to conduct a continual warfare with them. The Convention as an organization is famously unecumenical, but Baptist people are as open to fellowship with persons of other denominations as are the members of most denominations. Given their commitment to restricting "pulpit fellowship," as Pendleton and Graves called it, to fellow Baptists, the early Landmark leaders probably would be astonished to learn that in recent years the Convention has heard sermons by a Presbyterian, a Nazarene, an Eastern Orthodox, and an independent Bible church leader.

Local Baptist Congregations Should Keep Their Cooperation with Each Other to a Minimum

Since the Landmark Baptists claimed that Baptist churches are the only churches true to the New Testament, one might assume that they would want Baptist churches to work together very closely with each other. In fact, the opposite is true. Here is how they arrived at their surprising belief that cooperation among congregations should be minimal. They believed that local congregations are the only institutions mentioned in the New Testament. They pointed out that the New Testament never mentions organizations such as associations, conventions, mission boards, or publication boards. They also pointed out that in the New Testament the word *ekklesia* (church) is used to refer to a local congregation, and they insisted that it is never used to refer to all the congregations collectively; they themselves used the phrase "kingdom of God" to refer to the churches collectively. From the fact that local congregations are the only institutions mentioned in the New Testament, the Landmark Baptists drew the conclusion that the creation of other institutions is unbiblical. To be biblical, Baptists should not create other institutions, which meant that they should not attempt to cooperate with each other in order to sponsor missions or education or publications or benevolences.

While this may seem odd today when we are surrounded by large denominations, a case can be made for it. For example, it seems quite sensible to say that the decision about whether or not a person is suited to serve as a missionary ought to be made by that person's local congregation rather than by a mission board whose members and staff cannot possibly know the person as well as her fellow church members do. Further, local congregations are able to avoid the bureaucracies that are always found in large denominational organizations.

In a sense, the Landmark movement held a high view of local congregations. They felt that each congregation has a special status because it replicates the only institution mentioned in the New Testament. The Landmark Baptists saw two important implications in their principle of non-cooperation. One was that the denomination ought to have as few organizations as possible and keep them as small and powerless as possible. The other was that the Lord's Supper should be observed only in local congregations, and only members of the local congregation should participate in it.

Both of these ideas have influenced the Convention. The leaders of the Convention had to struggle against the Landmark influence in order to form the great organizations such as the Sunday School Board (now LifeWay Christian Resources). Today that struggle is over, and Southern Baptists are committed to the large organizations that make it possible for them to carry out ministries together that they could never carry out if the congregations refused to cooperate. As for the Lord's Supper, it is quite easy to see the influence of the Landmark Baptists upon the Southern Baptist Convention. The Convention was organized at a meeting held at the First Baptist Church of Augusta, Georgia, in 1845, a few years before the Landmark influence became dominant. When the messengers to Augusta gathered, they took the Lord's Supper together. Today it is unthinkable that the messengers at a meeting of the Southern Baptist Convention would take the Lord's Supper together.

With few exceptions, observances of the Lord's Supper in Southern Baptist life occur in local congregations. Most Baptists accept the Landmark interpretation that Jesus entrusted the ordinances, baptism and the Lord's Supper, to the churches rather than to the ordained clergy. However, most Southern Baptist churches do not accept the strict Landmark view that only members of a local congregation can take the Lord's Supper. Some Southern Baptist churches follow that practice, but many others offer the Lord's Supper to all baptized believers, and still others offer it to all Christians of whatever denomination.

Graves and his colleagues claimed that they were attempting to get Baptists to return to their true heritage; it is not a claim that historians today find plausible. There is considerable evidence that when Baptist churches were founded in the early seventeenth century, they made a great effort to express how much they had in common with other Christian churches. This was one of the purposes for which they adopted some of their confessions. Baptist historian Leon McBeth has written: "Baptists often used confessions not to proclaim 'Baptist distinctives' but instead to show how similar Baptists were to other orthodox Christians."[2] Also, the early Baptists were very committed to the idea that congregations should cooperate with each other, and they did not restrict participation in the Lord's Supper to members of a local congregation. Further, many interpreters today think that in Ephesians and elsewhere in the New Testament, the word *ekklesia* is used to refer to all churches collectively, and almost no interpreter today accepts the Landmark understanding of the phrase "kingdom of God."

The Landmark Baptists set up some landmarks, but they were new ones, not old ones; some of them are still standing in the Convention, but others are not.

Notes

[1] Leon McBeth, *The Baptist Heritage* (Nashville: Broadman Press, 1987), 60.

[2] Ibid., 68.

CHAPTER 8

DEEPER LIFE BELIEFS

All serious Christians are interested in Christian living, and thoughtful Christian leaders attempt to provide guidance and encouragement for all who want to live as faithful Christians. Across the centuries, the church has welcomed many varied insights concerning Christian living. With rare exceptions, no proposals concerning Christian living have been officially rejected by the church. The result of this openness is that quite diverse understandings of Christian living are to be found in the church across the centuries. The deeper life understanding is one of those.

In the middle of the nineteenth century, a distinctive understanding of Christian living was developed in the United States and Great Britain. It is usually called a holiness movement, although many insiders prefer to call it by the name of a very important early book which taught it, *The Higher Christian Life*. The book, published in 1859, was written by Presbyterian minister W. E. Boardman.[1] Other proponents of this particular understanding of Christian living were Hannah Whitall Smith and Robert Pearsall Smith. They taught that there is a second experience, distinct from conversion, by which a Christian may arrive at a state of holiness. In England the movement became known as the Keswick Movement because an important conference was held annually at Keswick in the Lake District. Antecedents for the holiness movement are found in the Methodist concern for personal holiness and in the work of the American evangelist Charles G. Finney.

The holiness movement of the nineteenth century gave birth to two new movements in the twentieth century. One is the Pentecostal movement, which began in Los Angeles early in the twentieth century under the leadership of a black holiness preacher, William J. Seymour.

Pentecostals follow the holiness teaching about a second experience distinct from conversion, and they add the idea that speaking in tongues is always given as a sign that one has had this experience. They call this experience "the baptism in the Holy Spirit." For half a century the Pentecostal movement existed in America in two groups of churches. One was the older holiness churches that accepted Pentecostalism, such as the Church of God (Cleveland, Tennessee); however, some holiness churches, such as the Church of God (Anderson, Indiana) and the Church of the Nazarene, resisted Pentecostalism. The second group of churches were the newly formed denominations such as the Assemblies of God.

Then, about the middle of the twentieth century, the Pentecostal movement spread beyond its own churches into all the churches, so that people who have the experiences of the baptism of the Spirit and of speaking in tongues may now be found in all denominations. This second phase is known as neo-Pentecostalism or the charismatic movement.

The second movement that descended from the nineteenth century holiness movement is the deeper life movement. It is very similar to the holiness movement, except for two things. First, unlike the original movement, this movement does not always emphasize that the second experience must be entirely distinct from the first; some persons move directly from their conversion experience to an experience of the deeper life. Second, in the deeper life movement the result of the second experience is not restricted to personal holiness. It is described as a deeper life, a higher life, and a victorious life, and it includes things such as inner peace, happiness, power in prayer and in witnessing, and success in one's work and family life. The deeper life is similar to Pentecostalism. The major difference between them is that Pentecostalism understands speaking in tongues to be the indispensable sign that one has received the baptism in the Spirit, and the deeper life does not.

Many Baptists who have embraced Pentecostalism and who speak in tongues have left the Convention, because the Convention has not been open to that experience. But none of those who have embraced the deeper life have felt any pressure to leave the Convention. This is a minority view that is welcomed in the Convention. Some of the leaders of the deeper life movement among Southern Baptists have been Peter Lord, Jack Taylor, and the late Bertha Smith and Jamie

Buckingham. The movement within the Convention is a loose net-
work of persons and organizations, and it maintains an attractive
publication entitled *Fullness*. Among Southern Baptists the deeper life
understanding of Christian living has been presented as four closely
related themes.

Many Christians Do Not Know the Secret of Christian Living

The deeper life movement teaches that there is a secret to living as a
faithful Christian. This secret is unknown not only to non-Christians
and to minimally committed Christians; it also is unknown to many
quite committed, serious Christians. Serious Christians who attempt to
live as faithful disciples will always fail if they do not know the secret of
Christian living.

Jack Taylor expresses this in a personal story. He says that he has
been through three stages in his life as a Christian. First, he thought it
was easy to be a good Christian, but he failed and became discouraged.
Then he made a discovery that moved him into a second stage: he discovered that it is very difficult to be a good Christian. He worked hard
to live as a faithful Christian, and once again he failed and became discouraged. Then he made a discovery that moved him into the third
stage: he discovered that it is impossible to be a good Christian. Only
with this discovery did he find the secret of a victorious life.[2]

The Secret Is That to Live the Christian Life
Christians Must Not Strive, but Depend upon God

Proponents of the deeper life recognize that many Christians do not
seriously attempt to live as faithful Christians, and this is an idea with
which most observers would agree. The doctrine of the deeper life goes
beyond simply living the Christian life. It teaches that it is a mistake for
committed Christians to attempt to live as faithful disciples. Christians
do not have within themselves the power to live faithfully. Only the
power of God is adequate for the impossible task of Christian living.
The attempt to live faithfully indicates that one is depending on one's
own power rather than on God's power.

The secret of victorious living, then, is to cease striving and
thereby to begin depending completely on God. Hannah Whitall
Smith, author of the immensely influential book *The Christian's Secret
of a Happy Life* (1875), described dependence on God as a move
toward passivity: "In order for a lump of clay to be made into a

beautiful vessel, it must be entirely abandoned to the potter, and must lie passive in his hands."[3]

When Christians Cease Striving and Depend upon God, God Will Work through Them

Once Christians have discovered the secret of Christian victory, they can begin to depend on God, and this opens the way for God to work through them and to do through them what they could never have done on their own. The deeper life movement speaks of the power of God in more or less the same terms that Christians have always used. It speaks of the power of the Spirit in one's life. It employs mystical phrases from the New Testament such as "Christ in you." In many ways, assurance is given that God will take control of the lives of dependent Christians and do wonderful things through them.

Christians Who Do Not Strive but Depend upon God Will Live Victoriously

The results of depending upon God are described in many ways. In the original holiness movement, the emphasis fell upon personal holiness or sanctification, that is, upon deliverance from personal sin and, in some cases, even from temptation. In the modern deeper life movement, a toned-down version of this idea is retained, and other emphases are added. Jack Taylor says of the key (the secret) to victorious living: "I have seen the key open the lock of personal disillusionment, marital disharmony, self condemnation, fear, anxiety, depression, and fling open the door upon a new and wonderful life!"[4]

The deeper life understanding of Christian living has a great goal and a great truth, and it provides a great help. Its *goal* is for Christians to experience God in their lives in ways that transform them. While some theologians and churches have minimized the experiential aspect of Christian faith, most believe that it is important to experience Christ's presence in one's life. The deeper life commitment to experiential religion is valuable.

Its great *truth* is that Christians are dependent upon God, which they sometimes forget in favor of independence. This feeling is close to pride, and it is neither realistic nor morally appropriate. The greatest saints have emphasized their need of God's help at every moment of their lives.

The great *help* that the deeper life understanding has provided for people is a resolution of the frustration Christians often feel when they have sincerely and conscientiously attempted to live faithfully and have failed. Apparently the apostle Paul had such an experience, for he wrote: "I don't do the good I want to do; instead, I do the evil that I do not want to do" (Rom 7:19). How are we to account for this experience? The deeper life has a clear answer: You tried to live faithfully and you failed because you tried in your own strength; if you will stop trying and begin depending completely upon God, then God will do through you what you clearly are unable to do for yourself.

This deeper life understanding has been an enormous help to many Christians and will continue to help many in the future. Nevertheless, we have some reservations about the understanding. First, the New Testament does not teach that there is a secret to Christian living. In fact, the idea that there is a secret is incompatible with the openness with which the New Testament writers presented their understandings of Christian life. The New Testament churches resisted gnosticism because it claimed to have a secret, arcane knowledge available only to an initiated elite.

Second, Christian living is not only a matter of passivity and dependence but also of activity and striving. The New Testament everywhere calls upon Christians to live obedient lives; all of this is written on the assumption that intentional obedience is possible and is a good thing. A popular hymn speaks of God's call to Christians to "Trust and Obey." This is a more balanced presentation than the deeper life message, "Depend, don't strive."

Third, it is not true that God begins to empower Christians only when they cease striving and begin to be totally dependent. Instead, the New Testament teaches that God is always providing the power that Christians need. God provides the gospel, which is the power of God unto salvation (Rom 1:16). God provides the church, which is the body of Christ through whom Jesus works in the world; all Christians are members of this body. God gives the Bible, which is the powerful Word of God (Heb 4:12) and which empowers Christians and provides them with guidance in their lives. God gives the Holy Spirit to live in the hearts of all Christians to guide and empower them. God gives all Christians spiritual gifts that empower them to serve God by serving the church. So it is a mistake to say that God works powerfully only in the lives of those who know a secret about dependence. The New

Testament teaches that God works powerfully in the lives of all Christians, all the time. Christians are to cooperate with God; that cooperation includes depending upon God, of course, but it also includes attempting to be obedient to God.

Fourth and finally, the deeper life movement no longer uses the explicit language of moral perfection, but underneath the language that is used in the movement lies an implicit promise of perfection upon earth. In its descriptions of the Christian life as deeper, higher, overcoming, victorious, happy, and a life of fullness, the movement hints at the possibility of perfection.[5] The writers of the New Testament, like most of the church across the centuries, understood that perfection is a promise that will be fulfilled for Christians in the life to come and a standard toward which they are to strive in the present life, but it is not a state at which they can arrive in this life. Most Christians have identified with the apostle Paul when he wrote, "I do not claim that I have already succeeded or have already become perfect. I keep striving to win the prize for which Christ Jesus has already won me to himself" (Phil 3:12).

The appeal of the deeper life among Southern Baptists has been great. A vocal and influential minority of Southern Baptists has accepted all four of its teachings and has propagated them effectively. Nevertheless, this remains a minority view among Southern Baptists, and there are millions of Southern Baptists who have never even heard of this interpretation of Christian living.

Notes

[1]W. E. Boardman, *The Higher Christian Life* (Boston: Henry Hoyt, 1859).

[2]Jack R. Taylor, *The Key to Triumphant Living* (Nashville: Broadman Press, 1971).

[3]Quoted in Daniel G. Reid et al., eds., *Dictionary of Christianity in America* (Downers Grove: InterVarsity Press, 1990), 1096.

[4]Jack R. Taylor, *The Key to Triumphant Living*, 27.

[5]Ibid., 16.

CHAPTER 9

FUNDAMENTALIST BELIEFS

Throughout most of the nineteenth century, the various Protestant denominations spent a lot of time and energy arguing against each other; we have seen how Landmark Baptists did this vigorously. But to some extent that changed when a new theology arose in the nineteenth century, a product of the Enlightenment. It was called "liberal Protestantism," and it took several different forms. As it became stronger in the United States in the late nineteenth century, traditionalists in all the Protestant denominations came to see it as a threat. Consequently, some of them set aside their denominational differences in order to form a loose coalition to act as a united front against their common enemy, liberalism. Curtis Lee Laws, a Baptist newspaper editor, coined the term "fundamentalist" to describe his fellow traditionalists who were defending traditional faith against liberalism, and "fundamentalism" soon came to be used for a loose coalition of traditionalists from many denominations who united in order to fight liberalism.

Fundamentalism itself quickly became a threat to many other Protestants, and they reacted to it. Some, such as Harry Emerson Fosdick, urged the churches to resist fundamentalism; he preached a famous sermon entitled "Shall the Fundamentalists Win?" in which he urged resistance. Other persons, such as the journalist H. L. Mencken, spoke contemptuously of fundamentalists as "Neanderthals." The contempt of Mencken and others has stuck; the word "fundamentalist" still carries connotations of contempt. The word is used in this chapter only for those persons who lived earlier in the century and who referred to themselves as fundamentalists. Later it will be pointed out that some people today hold some of the same beliefs that people such as Curtis Lee Laws held. This will be done only in order to understand the views better, not to express contempt for those who hold them.

A conventional interpretation of fundamentalism is that it was the religion of a marginal group of rural, uneducated, Southern Protestants. This proposal is interesting because it is wrong on every count. Fundamentalism was stronger in the North than in the South, stronger in cities than in rural areas, and many of its leaders, at least in its early period, were intellectuals such as J. Gresham Machen.[1]

Several scholars have studied fundamentalism carefully and have helped us all to understand it more accurately. They have offered several interpretations of fundamentalist theology. Ernest Sandeen proposed that fundamentalism was formed by the merger of two previously separate theological traditions.[2] One was a tradition that affirmed the inerrancy of the original manuscripts of the Bible, proposed by theologians at Princeton Theological Seminary such as Charles Hodge and B. B. Warfield. The other was a tradition of dispensationalism and premillennialism associated with the Bible schools such as Moody Bible Institute. What is interesting about this proposal is that, prior to the formation of the fundamentalist coalition, these two groups had uneasy relationships with each other. The Princeton theologians were emphatically opposed to the premillennialism of the Bible schools, and the Bible school leaders emphasized the King James Version of the Bible rather than the original Hebrew and Greek manuscripts emphasized by the Princeton theologians. Nevertheless, these two groups joined forces in order to resist their common enemy, liberalism. More recently, George Marsden has proposed that two other theological strands were also part of the tapestry of fundamentalism. One was revivalism and the other was the deeper life movement. Both were closely associated with the great evangelist D. L. Moody (d. 1899). Marsden is surely right: fundamentalism emphasizes conversion and evangelism as much as it does other beliefs.[3]

In order to understand fundamentalism, it also is necessary to remember the common commitment that brought together these people who earlier had been divided along denominational and other lines, namely, their determination to resist liberalism. They did not organize simply in order to create a fellowship from which liberals would be excluded; they organized to create a common front for a battle against liberalism. We may, therefore, think of fundamentalism as the bringing together of four separate theological traditions and of a new component. The new component was militant resistance to theological liberalism, and the four traditions were revivalism, the deeper life understanding of Christian living, the inerrancy of the original manuscripts of the Bible, and premillennialism.

In earlier chapters we have reviewed revivalism and the deeper life movement. We now turn our attention to the other three themes.

True Christians Should Oppose Liberalism Militantly

George Dollar is a historian who has taught at Bob Jones University, which is in some ways the flagship institution of fundamentalism. He is the author of a large and indispensable history of fundamentalism titled *A History of Fundamentalism in America*. In it he defines "fundamentalism" as follows: "Historical Fundamentalism is the literal exposition of all the affirmations and attitudes of the Bible and the militant exposure of all non-Biblical affirmations and attitudes."[4] The word "militant" is important. Dollar believed that a fundamentalist must not only believe what the Bible teaches, teach what the Bible teaches, and oppose teachings contrary to the Bible, but also be *militant* in opposing teachings contrary to the Bible. From the point of view of a fundamentalist, it is morally wrong to believe the Bible and then refuse to be militant in one's opposition to unbiblical teachings. A text much loved by fundamentalists is: "Earnestly contend for the faith which was once delivered unto the saints" (Jude 3, KJV).

In Dollar's sense, most Southern Baptists did not become fundamentalists. It is true that some Southern Baptists leaders contributed to the collection of booklets called *The Fundamentals*, one of the defining documents of the fundamentalist movement. It is also true that Southern Baptists are a traditional Protestant group. But in the 1920s and 1930s, the Southern Baptists rejected proposals from some of their leaders that they should become militant in their opposition to liberalism. One famous Southern Baptist pastor attempted to lead Southern Baptists to become militant. He was J. Frank Norris, pastor of the First Baptist Church of Fort Worth, Texas. Many Southern Baptists believed his message that some of the schools of the Convention were becoming liberal, many worried about it, and some limited actions were taken concerning alleged liberalism among Southern Baptists. The important decision of the Convention was to follow not the leadership of Norris but that of George W. Truett, pastor of the First Baptist Church of Dallas. In 1924 Norris's church was expelled from the Baptist General

Convention of Texas, and in 1927 Truett was elected president of the Southern Baptist Convention.

The logic of fundamentalism is very persuasive. It says that, since God gives us truth, we ought not only to believe it and to teach it but to fight for it. What could be wrong with that? The answer, of course, is that militancy toward other Christians, however mistaken they may be in their theology, destroys the church and undermines the church's evangelistic message to the world. Once the fighting begins, people become suspicious of one another and angry at one another. Militancy destroys cooperation and fellowship. This is especially serious for Southern Baptists, many of whom do not have a theology about the universal church or about Christian unity that would act to keep them together during a fight. Cooperation, trust, and fellowship are the only ties that bind them to one another, and if these fail, the Convention has nothing to fall back on to keep it together.

The Original Manuscripts of the Bible Were Inerrant

In chapter 1 we observed that Christians across the centuries have agreed that the Bible is the uniquely inspired Word of God and that it is authoritative for the faith and life of Christians, and in chapter 2 we observed that one of the insights of the Protestant reformation was that the Bible alone is the written Word of God. Across the centuries Christians have used words such as "infallible" (unfailing) and "inerrant" (unerring) to describe the Bible. When, therefore, in the nineteenth century some liberal Protestant scholars came to the conclusion that the Bible contains errors, conservative scholars naturally set out to refute this view, and some of them, particularly at Princeton Theological Seminary, adopted a new strategy for doing so. They acknowledged that some errors may exist in the texts and translations of the Bible that we have today, including the beloved King James Version, but they argued that these errors came into modern texts and translations during the process of transmission of the Bible. The original Hebrew and Greek manuscripts, they insisted, contained no errors of any kind.

Many Christians are not familiar with the fascinating story of the transmission of the Bible. The oldest parts of the Bible were written more than a thousand years before Christ and the latest parts several decades after Christ. For about fourteen centuries after Christ, all copies of the Bible were handwritten. Printing by moveable type was invented in Europe about the middle of the fifteenth century. Johannes Gutenberg, the inventor of the new process, published his great Bible in 1460. Naturally, many of the handwritten copies of the Bible contain slight variations. Even though we do not have any of the original manuscripts of the Bible, biblical scholars are very skilled at retrieving what the writers of the Bible originally wrote, so much so that we may have great confidence in the texts we have today. Nevertheless, many variations do appear in the texts that were copied by hand before the invention of printing.

In the nineteenth century, scholars at Princeton Theological Seminary and elsewhere began to argue that, even though modern texts and translations of the Bible might contain errors, the original manuscripts of the Bible did not contain any errors, even small errors concerning trivial matters. The leaders of the fundamentalist movement routinely employed the strategy of defending the truth of the Bible by appealing to the original manuscripts. The original manuscripts are called the "autographs," which means "the writings themselves," and everyone agrees that they were all lost centuries ago; they do not exist today. That is why I used the past tense in stating this theme: "The original manuscripts of the Bible were inerrant."

The Princeton theology also put a new twist on the traditional Christian conviction that the Bible is truthful. It extended the truthfulness of the Bible to matters of history and science as well as to faith and morals; it affirmed the truthfulness of the Bible in all details as well as in its great message. However, as we have seen, it restricted its claim for the truthfulness of the Bible to the original manuscripts, and it was content to say that the texts and translations we have today are true only to the extent that these accurately present what was written in the original manuscripts.

Biblical inerrancy in this technical sense was much debated in the 1970s and 1980s. Many books were written to defend the idea and others to refute it, and an International Council on Biblical Inerrancy was formed to defend it. The Council issued three well-known statements about the Bible, one of which has become a benchmark of the meaning of biblical inerrancy today — "The Chicago Statement on Biblical Inerrancy."[5] It is a sophistical, nuanced, technical statement, and many scholars feel that it offers the best model for affirming the truthfulness of the Bible in our time.

Some Southern Baptist scholars accept the modern, technical understanding of biblical inerrancy, and others do not.[6] Since 1979, those who have accepted this idea have been assuming leadership in the Convention, and one result is that the idea is now more widely known and discussed than it was before 1979. A sophisticated and winsome presentation of that view was disseminated among Southern Baptists as the annual doctrinal study book in 1992.[7] As might be expected, the new technical vocabulary of inerrancy of the autographs is not found in *The Baptist Faith and Message*. The first section of that document contains an affirmation that the Bible has "God for its author, salvation for its end, and truth without any mixture of error for its matter." Two things may be said about this statement. First, since there is no reference in *The Baptist Faith and Message* to the autographs, it is natural to understand this as an affirmation of the Bible we now have, that is, of modern texts and translations of the Bible. Second, the phrase "for its matter" is ambiguous; it could refer to every detail in the Bible, or it could be understood as a reference to the general message of the Bible. There is no reference to matters of science and history in *The Baptist Faith and Message*, and a sentence in the preface says that "the sole authority for faith and practice among Baptists is the Scriptures of the Old and New Testaments." In view of this, it seems natural to interpret the phrase "its matter" as a reference to issues of "faith and practice" rather than to all of the details in the Bible.

Christ Will Return to Earth and Rule for a Thousand Years

In chapter 1 we saw that hope is an indispensable component of the Christian tradition and that it is shared by all Christians. Christians have always had hope for both the present world and the world to come. The customary word for referring to the Christian hope for the world to come is "heaven," and the customary phrase for referring to the Christian hope for the present world is "the kingdom of God."

In the nineteenth century, many Christians began to employ another word for their hope for the present world, the word "millennium," which means "thousand years." The word does not occur in the Bible, but in Revelation 20:1-10 there are six references to a thousand-year rule of Christ. During the nineteenth century some biblical scholars, especially in Britain and the United States, emphasized the millennium in their teaching, and people in many churches came to feel that the millennium is the best way to express the Christian hope concerning this world and its end. That was the dominant view in the fundamentalist movement.

Three general understandings of the millennium are available. One is that the thousand years referred to in Revelation are a symbol, perhaps for the church or for heaven. This view is supported by the fact that the book of Revelation contains many symbols. This view is called *amillennialism,* which means "no millennium," because it does not interpret Revelation to refer to a literal thousand-year reign of Christ upon earth.

The second view is *postmillennialism.* It was the dominant view in many churches in the nineteenth century, presenting the millennium as a reign of Christ upon earth. However, it sees that reign as spiritual rather than literal. Postmillennialism teaches that the Spirit will guide and empower the church to do its work in the world so that more and more of the world will come to have faith in Christ, and Christ's reign will be extended over most of the people on earth, resulting in an era of peace and progress, of faith and justice. That era is the millennium, and it will be completed by Christ returning in person to the earth and accepting the homage that almost all of the world will then wish to give him. Postmillennialism is a very positive view, and it empowered much of the great missionary movement of the nineteenth century. It received its most serious setback with the global traumas of the twentieth century. The World Wars, the great depression, and other expressions of evil in the world make it difficult to believe that the world is making progress in the way postmillennialists had thought.

The third view is *premillennialism,* and it became very popular in the twentieth century. It is pessimistic about the possibility of progress in the world. It pictures the world as getting worse and worse, and even the church as becoming less and less faithful to Christ. Moral decline will continue until the moment when Christ suddenly returns and establishes his kingdom on earth. There are two kinds of premillennialism. The historic type, held by many Christians across the centuries, is simply that Christ will suddenly return to earth and establish his rule for a thousand years; he will then judge the world, and history will come to an end.

In the nineteenth century, certain biblical scholars developed a more elaborate understanding of premillennialism. It is called *dispensational premillennialism,* and it is well represented by a study Bible which was written by C. I. Scofield early in the twentieth century. Scofield believed that God has related to human beings differently in different ages, or dispensations; he located seven dispensations in the Bible. He developed his understanding of the end of the world against this background. He attempted to piece together what is said about the future of the world in various texts of the Old and New Testaments, and he understood the future to be as follows. First, the world will continue to degenerate. Then, when no one expects it (though there are signs pointing to it), Christ will come in the sky (not to the earth) and take up all Christians, living and dead, to be with him; this is the rapture of the church. Then, for seven years the earth will experience the most awful suffering in human history; this is the great tribulation. Next, Christ will return to earth with his church and will establish himself as the ruler of the world, and he will imprison Satan. Christ will rule the earth for a thousand years; that is the millennium. Then, Satan will be released and will gather his people together, and Christ will gather his people together, and they will fight a great battle; this is called Armageddon. Christ will, of course, defeat his enemies. Then he will judge all people and send each one either to heaven or to hell for eternity.

Dispensational premillennialism became popular with many Southern Baptists in the twentieth century, so much so that many are surprised to learn that premillennialism has not always been the dominant view among Baptists. Baptist confessions of faith are quite neutral about the details of the end of the world. *The Baptist Faith and Message* (X) says noncommittally, "God, in his own time and in his own way, will bring the world to its appropriate end. According to his promise, Jesus Christ will return personally and visibly in glory to the earth." This noncommittal view is expressed also in a slogan that is popular with many Baptists, namely, that when it comes to the return of Christ, it is best to stay off the planning committee and to serve on the welcoming committee.

These, then, are three themes held by the fundamentalist coalition that was formed in the United States early in the twentieth century, which have been embraced by a minority of Southern Baptists: militant opposition to liberalism, inerrancy of the non-extant, original manuscripts of the Bible, and dispensational premillennialism.

Notes

[1]Note the respect with which Machen is treated by that least religious of American social critics, Walter Lippman, in *A Preface to Morals* (New York: The Macmillan Company, 1929), 31-34. Mark Noll reviewed the change of leadership in fundamentalism in *Between Faith and Criticism: Evangelicals, Scholarship, and the Bible in America* (San Francisco: Harper & Row, 1986).

[2]Ernest Sandeen, *The Roots of Fundamentalism* (Chicago: University of Chicago Press, 1970).

[3]George Marsden, *Fundamentalism and American Culture* (Oxford: Oxford University Press, 1980).

[4]George Dollar, *A History of Fundamentalism in America* (Greenville: Bob Jones University Press, n.d.). The definition of "fundamentalism" appears in large, bold type on an unnumbered page at the front of the book.

[5]"The Chicago Statement on Biblical Inerrancy" (Walnut Creek, CA: The International Council on Biblical Inerrancy, n.d. [1978]).

[6]See *The Unfettered Word: Southern Baptists Confront the Authority-Inerrancy Question*, Robison B. James, ed. (Waco: Word Books, 1987); *Baptists and the Bible*, L. Russ Bush and Tom J. Nettles (Chicago: Moody Press, 1980); *The Proceedings of the Conference on Biblical Inerrancy*, Michael Smith, ed. (Nashville: Broadman Press, 1987); and "Biblical Inerrancy: Pro or Con?" in *The Theological Educator*, David S. Dockery and Philip D. Wise (Spring 1988), 15-44.

[7]David S. Dockery, *The Doctrine of the Bible* (Nashville: Convention Press, 1991). This series of doctrinal study books includes an equally winsome volume that presents a high view of Scripture in a more traditional and less technical form; see Russell H. Dilday, Jr., *The Doctrine of Biblical Authority* (Nashville: Convention Press, 1982).

CHAPTER 10

PROGRESSIVE BELIEFS

We have considered five sets of beliefs held by minorities in the Southern Baptist Convention. All of them come from the right side of the Convention; that is, they can claim with some degree of plausibility to be traditional Baptist beliefs. The beliefs to be reviewed in the present chapter come from the left rather than the right side of the Convention. They are not presented as part of the Baptist tradition that has been lost and needs to be retrieved, but rather are acknowledged by their sponsors to be new proposals that, the sponsors say, are appropriate for the life of the Convention in the future.

The beliefs described in each of the previous five chapters were closely tied together so that, for example, a person who held one of the Calvinist beliefs was likely to hold all of them. The beliefs to be described in the present chapter are not closely tied to each other, and there are Baptists who hold one or two of these beliefs but not the others. Each of these beliefs is discrete. This means that the sequence in which they are presented is unimportant.

It is customary for those who reject the beliefs described in the present chapter to refer to them as "liberal." I have employed the word "progressive" rather than the word "liberal" because the beliefs are not all associated with liberal Protestantism, and also because, in the United States today, in both political and religious discourse, the word "liberal" is usually pejorative.

Women Should Be Ordained and Serve as Ministers

The story of the place of women in the life of Southern Baptists has been told by H. Leon McBeth and others.[1] It is a story whose outline is similar to that of the place of women in American public life generally. Early in the life of the Convention, women were not allowed to serve as messengers to the Convention.[2] Women did not serve as pastors of churches. Even so, they were active in many areas of Southern Baptist life, and, in fact, they bore much of the burden of ministry in many local churches. They served as missionaries, and they organized societies for securing missions support in the United States and abroad. They were church musicians and teachers of children and youth.

Women first attended the Convention as messengers in 1877. Even before that time, they had formed the Woman's Missionary Union, an organization of their own devoted to missions education and support that met simultaneously with the annual meeting of the Convention. In 1905, a woman addressed the Convention for the first time. Women were allowed to vote in the Convention beginning in 1918, two years before women were allowed to vote in American political elections. The first woman chosen as an officer of the Convention was Marie Mathis, who was elected second vice-president in 1963.[3]

In many small ways, women have become more involved in the life of the Convention and more influential in the Convention. The big step, the most difficult one, concerned ordination to serve as a pastor. That step seems to have been taken first in 1964.[4] Ordination is conducted among Southern Baptists by local congregations, not by associations or conventions. There are no mandates from the denomination about whom to ordain. This means that each local congregation can decide for itself whether or not to ordain a woman. Most have not ordained women and would not do so under any circumstances, but some have. The number of ordained Southern Baptist women is now several hundred. Many of these serve as military chaplains for whom ordination is required. All Southern Baptist chaplains are endorsed by the North American Mission Board.

Very few women have been called to serve as pastors of Southern Baptist churches. Those who oppose an expanded role for women in the Convention have drawn a line at the point of ordaining women to serve as pastors. Here is an eloquent expression of opposition to the ordination of women pastors:

Ordination says to the world that the church is placing the highest authority of the ordaining church in the hands of the person being ordained. Since Scripture states that "I do not permit a woman to teach or to have authority over a man" (1 Tim 2:11), the ruling pastor-teacher should be a man. The pastor-teacher should be in complete authority over the public worship service. At his discretion a woman may be called on to pray, to give testimony, but it should be done with respect to the pastor's position, not to take over the service.[5]

Those who favor the ordination of women to serve as pastors see no reasons to draw any lines about how women may serve in the churches. They understand the New Testament passages such as the one that Mrs. Kaemmerling quoted to have been God's will in the setting of the first century, when a woman's exercise of public leadership would have created a scandal and so hindered the work of the gospel. However, they feel that in the setting of the modern world, where women routinely exercise public leadership in business, government, and the professions, it creates a scandal and hinders the work of the gospel for the church to exclude women from a similar role in the church.

There is another issue here also, namely, the issue of authority. Objections to the ordination of women often are premised on the idea that ordination is a conferral of authority. But is it? There are three basic understandings of the theological meaning of ordination in the church.[6] The Roman Catholic understanding is that ordination confers an indelible grace that authorizes a man to offer the Mass. The magisterial Reformation understanding is that ordination confers the authority to preach the gospel. The third understanding rejects both of the others and defines ordination as the giving of a communal blessing to a person who feels called to service and is willing to follow that call. The third understanding is more compatible with the Baptist theological heritage than the others. Nevertheless, those who have resisted the ordination of women to serve as pastors have spoken repeatedly in terms of the second view.

The Bible Should Be Studied Critically

The story of the rise of biblical criticism in the nineteenth century has been told many times. The Southern Baptists, like many other

Christian groups, initially resisted much of the critical study of the Bible. Eventually many Southern Baptists came to accept textual criticism, the attempt to reconstruct the best Hebrew and Greek texts of the Bible. However, other forms of criticism, such as source criticism, form criticism, and redaction criticism, are still resisted by many Southern Baptists.

A minority of Southern Baptists have proposed that all responsible criticism be accepted. The argument in support of this view is that the Bible is a human book as well as a divine book, and that the human dimension means that the Bible should be studied in the same way any other book from the ancient world should be studied. More important, the argument is that the critical study of the Bible helps the church to understand the message of the Bible, which is the goal of Bible study. Some have also argued that critical Bible study serves a conservative function, namely, that it acts as a constraint on bizarre interpretations of the Bible.

Many Southern Baptists, like many people in other denominations, do not know what biblical criticism is. When they hear the phrase "criticism of the Bible," they ask, "Why would any Christian want to criticize the Bible?" The phrase is certainly an unhappy one, and this led one great Southern Baptist teacher, C. Penrose St. Amant, to propose that the phrase "biblical criticism" be replaced with "biblical analysis."[7] What is biblical criticism? This is an essentially contested concept.[8] In my judgment the most helpful insight is that the study of any text becomes critical when one moves beyond learning from the texts and begins to generate questions of one's own to put to the text.[9] This definition helps us to recognize that even though many Christians oppose biblical criticism on principle, many of them have nevertheless benefited from it, and not only at the level of textual criticism. For example, conservative teachers are quite as likely as more progressive ones to begin their teaching about a book of the Bible with information about the book's authorship, date, and purpose. These things are the result of asking our questions, not those of the authors. The biblical authors did not, for example, intend to tell us the date of their writing. The study by which we learn this is therefore critical study in the sense given above, and it is employed by biblical scholars of all kinds.

Two things remain to be said. One is that the resistance of conservative scholars to biblical criticism often is a resistance to particular conclusions reached by particular biblical critics. For example, for a very long time many biblical critics believed that John's Gospel was produced by a Gentile with no appreciation for the Jewishness of Jesus and his message. Naturally this view disturbed those who felt that the Gospel was, as it claimed to be, apostolic. As it turned out, the critics were wrong, and the Jewishness of the fourth Gospel is now accepted by biblical scholars.[10]

The other thing to be said is that fewer and fewer scholars are prepared to defend the idea that biblical criticism is the only form of Bible study. Criticism is a relatively modern development, and many scholars are now at work retrieving the kinds of Bible study the church did before the advent of criticism. In fact, Andrew Louth, a learned theologian formerly of Oxford University, has even made a case for the usefulness of the allegorical study of the Bible.[11] While this is an extreme view, it is clear that many Bible scholars are now open to the idea that criticism should accept its place as one of several methods of Bible study. Among Southern Baptists, however, it remains true that those who promote the critical study of the Bible remain a progressive minority.

The Best Higher Education Is Exploration Not Indoctrination

For purposes of analysis, we may think of higher education, including theological education, as existing on a range with four principal options. The options, moving from right to left, are brainwashing, indoctrination, exploration, and relativization. Brainwashing is a coercive form of education that overwhelms students and force-feeds them information they are in no position to resist. No one in Southern Baptist life promotes brainwashing.

Indoctrination is not coercive. It is carried out on the assumption that the primary purpose of education is the faithful transmission of a heritage by teachers to students. This transmission includes active resistance to every view that contests the heritage. If teachers refer to views that contest the heritage, it is only to refute them and to show the superiority of the heritage. Indoctrination sometimes includes a fortress mentality, motivated by a fear of the dangerous ideas to be found outside the heritage. Furthermore, faithfulness to the heritage is sometimes equated with faithfulness to Christ; as a consequence, any view that contests the heritage must be unfaithful to Christ, and this leads to very intense reactions to people who hold such views. Many Southern Baptists believe that indoctrination is the best education.

The third view is that the best education is exploration. Like the second view, it supports the idea that education includes the transmission of a tradition, because it believes that the tradition contains truth that students need. However, this view is open to the presence of truth outside the heritage and to views that contest the heritage. In this kind of education students are challenged to develop a critical appreciation for the tradition and a critical appreciation for views contesting the tradition, and they are entrusted with the responsibility of deciding for themselves which view is truthful. In this kind of higher education the clash of views is understood not as a conspiracy to subvert the truth, but as the honorable effort of finite, fallible human beings to understand the truth, a project that often exceeds everyone's grasp. Proponents of this view do not equate unfaithfulness to the theological tradition with unfaithfulness to Christ or condemn those who do not accept all of the heritage as unfaithful Christians.

Many Southern Baptists believe that exploration is the best understanding of higher education. They feel that indoctrination does only half of the work that educators ideally ought to be doing. As much as they respect the traditions to be transmitted, they do not want to stop there but to encourage students to explore beyond the boundaries of the tradition.

Finally, there is a relativistic understanding of higher education. On this understanding education does not include the transmission of any particular tradition. The truth is to be found, it says, only in the interaction of our minds with the developing future, not in any heritage from the past. When the truth is found, it is unstable and apt to change; it is relative to the changing situation, not absolute or changeless. No one in Southern Baptist life holds this understanding of education.

Among Southern Baptists, then, the two live options concerning higher education are indoctrination — the transmission of a heritage only — and exploration — the transmission of a heritage together with an exploration of other sources in the quest for truth and understanding. Indoctrination necessarily excludes a factor that exploration necessarily includes, so there is no way to hold both views. Both of these positions are held by responsible Southern Baptists.

Unfortunately, discussions about exploration and indoctrination are often misleading. On the one hand, those who are committed to education as exploration sometimes charge those who are committed to indoctrination with believing in brainwashing; it is an untrue accusation. On the other hand, those who believe in indoctrination sometimes charge those committed to exploration with relativism; this also is an untrue accusation. These untrue accusations must be set aside in order for a meaningful engagement to occur between the two views.

Baptists Should Participate in Ecumenism

With the possible exception of the Pentecostal and charismatic movements, the ecumenical movement, the movement toward Christian unity, was the most dramatic worldwide development in the church during the twentieth century. Ecumenism was born among Protestant missionaries. On the mission field, it did not make much sense to set up several varieties of Protestant churches among people who were unclear about what Christianity is. The Eastern Orthodox are very committed to ecumenism, and in the 1960s the Roman Catholic Church committed itself to ecumenism.

When the ecumenical movement was born early in the twentieth century, some Southern Baptists showed significant interest in interdenominational relations. In the end, however, the more isolationist approach won out among the Southern Baptists, and they took the lead in forming a new organization, the Baptist World Alliance, as an alternative to groups such as the National Council of Churches in America and the World Council of Churches. They have continued to refuse to participate in most ecumenical organizations. There are limited exceptions. For example, the Convention participates in the International Sunday School Lesson program, and it has always been friendly to the American Bible Society. But the Convention has avoided most ties with non-Baptist organizations, including ecumenical ones. However, a minority of Southern Baptists has been troubled by this. Their study of the New Testament passages that speak of the unity of Christ's followers, especially of the great prayer of Jesus for the unity of all his disciples (John 17), has led them to believe in the unity of all Christians and to be willing to live out that belief in practical ways. They have come to believe that an important expression is through participation in ecumenical bodies. Most Southern Baptists are not convinced. They feel that it is important for the Convention to continue to avoid entanglements with non-Baptists.

This is not quite the whole story, however. The Christian church has been changing in America, and some of the changes make it more difficult for Southern Baptists or anyone else not to encounter people in other denominations. Through Christian radio, television, and other media, many Southern Baptists have come to appreciate the work of many non-Baptists. And, of course, Southern Baptist people have always had friends who were devout Christians in other denominations.

The situation in the Convention, therefore, is not so much between a conservative group who want to avoid contacts with non-Baptists and a progressive group who want to make such contacts. It is rather between a conservative group who want to make contacts with one set of non-Baptists and a progressive group who want to make contacts with a different set of non-Baptists.

Here, then, are four views that are held by a minority of Southern Baptists and are representative of the progressive impulse: Women should be ordained to serve as pastors, the Bible should be studied critically, education should be exploration rather than indoctrination, and Baptists should participate in ecumenical activities.

Summary

Let us imagine a star surrounded by six planets. The star represents the beliefs held by the majority of Southern Baptists until 1979, and the planets represent six clusters of beliefs held by visible minorities in the Convention until 1979. If we described the majority tradition in a way that represents how these beliefs are lived out in the life of a Baptist church and in the experiences of Baptists, it might sound as follows.

In the background of Southern Baptist beliefs are the ideas that there is one God and that God created the world. The world has fallen into sin, so the Father sent the Son into the world to save sinners. Jesus Christ died for the sins of the world and rose again. The greatest decision in every person's life is what to do about Jesus Christ. God wants everyone to be saved, and everyone can be saved by putting his or her faith in Christ. Those who are saved are secure in the salvation God gives them, and they can have complete assurance that their eternal home is heaven. All those who are saved should participate actively in the life of a church. God has called the church to carry out a world mission, and, with the help of the Holy Spirit, the church can win the world to Christ. The most important part of the church's work is missions and evangelism, and to carry these out, the church must preach the gospel and work vigorously to persuade people to respond to Christ with faith.

A true church is a believers church comprising saved persons who have been immersed in water in the name of the Father, the Son, and the Holy Spirit. Those who have been baptized thereby become members of the church and may receive the Lord's Supper. Believers churches are self-governing congregations, and they seek the will of God without interference from anyone outside the congregation. All Christians are priests, and they make their church decisions by democratic means. They also cooperate voluntarily with other congregations to carry out missions, evangelism, education, and benevolences. The churches should accept no support from government; the Baptist ideal is a free church in a free state. Christians confidently hope that in the future God will complete this great work in the world. The Bible is God's written, authoritative Word to guide Christians in their common faith and life, the only written revelation given by God.

That is the star, the majority tradition. We turn now to the six planets rotating around it, the minority traditions.

The first planet represents the *Anabaptist tradition.* It reacts against the church status of Southern Baptists and calls them to return to a sect status by resisting the temptation to be powerful in the ways of the world. It calls them to follow the teachings of Jesus in the Sermon on the Mount and become pacifists. And it calls them to revise their understanding of justice to include the idea that justice requires that every person has enough food, clothing, housing, education, and job opportunities to live a decent life.

The second tradition is the *Calvinist*; its concerns are related to salvation. It calls Southern Baptists to a distinctive understanding of God's sovereignty: God sovereignly chooses to save some people and to damn others. God intended that Christ's death would benefit not the entire world, but only the elect who are chosen for salvation. Because people are dead in their sins, they are unable to have faith in Christ until after they have been given new life by God. God works in the lives of the elect in such a way that they are finally unable to resist God's grace.

The third minority tradition is the *Landmark*; its concerns are related to the church. It insists that Baptist churches are the only truly

New Testament churches, and it calls them to dissociate themselves from those who baptize infants. It urges Baptists to keep cooperation among local congregations to a minimum. One expression of this is to invite to the Lord's Supper only those who are members of the local congregation in which the supper is being observed.

The fourth minority tradition is the *deeper life*; its concerns are for Christian living. It deals with the disappointments that all sensitive Christians feel concerning how they live their lives by saying that the problem is that many Christians, even informed and dedicated ones, do not know the secret of Christian living. The secret is that they must cease striving to live as faithful Christians and begin instead to depend upon God. When they do this, God will work in their lives, and the result will be lives that are always characterized by victory and happiness.

A fifth minority tradition is the *fundamentalist*. Fundamentalism calls Southern Baptists not only to believe in the fundamentals of the Christian faith and to teach them, but also to defend them militantly against all enemies, especially against liberalism. It urges them to recognize that the original Hebrew and Greek manuscripts of the Bible, which no longer exist, were inerrant in all matters including science and history as well as faith and morals. It encourages Baptists to fill out their understanding of the end of the world with more than an affirmation that the end is in God's hands. It calls for affirmations concerning the tribulation, the millennium, and the battle of Armageddon.

The final planet represents a set of *non-traditional* proposals for Southern Baptists to adopt several unrelated, progressive activities. One is to ordain women to serve as pastors of churches. Another is to use all critical methods along with other methods of Bible study. A third is to include exploration in its higher education. And a fourth is to enter into ecumenical relationships with all kinds of Christians.

This is my reconstruction of Southern Baptist theology in the years leading up to 1979. It is the way we were.

It is no longer the way we are.

Notes

[1]H. Leon McBeth, *Women in Baptist Life* (Nashville: Broadman Press, 1979).

[2]For details, see Juliette Mather, "Women, Convention Privileges of" in *Encyclopedia of Southern Baptists* (Nashville: Broadman Press, 1958), II, 1542-44.

[3]See Catherine B. Allen, "Women's Movements and Southern Baptists" in *Encyclopedia of Southern Baptists* (Nashville: Broadman Press, 1982), IV, 2560-62.

[4]See C. Anne Davis, "Women, Ordination of Southern Baptist" in *Encyclopedia of Southern Baptists*, IV, 2557-58.

[5]Charlene Kaemmerling, "Ordination of Women: Wrong or Right?" in *The Theological Educator* (Spring 1988), 98-99.

[6]See Marjorie Warkentin, *Ordination: A Biblical-Historical View* (Grand Rapids: William B. Eerdmans Publishing Company, 1982).

[7]"Southern Baptist Theology Today: An Interview with C. Penrose St. Amant" in *The Theological Educator* (Spring 1982), 16.

[8]For the meaning of an essentially contested concept, see W. B. Gaillie, *Philosophy and the Historical Understanding* (New York: Schocken Books, 1964), 157ff.

[9]For this understanding of criticism, see R. G. Collingwood, *The Idea of History* (Oxford: Oxford University Press, 1956), 269-70.

[10]See Stephen Neill, *The Interpretation of the New Testament, 1861–1961* (London: Oxford University Press, 1966), 315ff. Neill tells a story about how the orthodox Jewish scholar, Dr. Israel Abrahams, who was Reader in Rabbinics at Cambridge, once startled a learned society by remarking that "to us Jews the Fourth Gospel is the most Jewish of the four."

[11]Andrew Louth, *Discerning the Mystery: An Essay on the Nature of Theology* (Oxford: Clarendon Press, 1983), Chapter V.

PART THREE

THE WAY
WE MAY
BECOME

CHAPTER ELEVEN

THE WAY WE MAY BECOME: LOST TRADITIONS

From the beginning of this book we have attempted to emphasize that the controversy in the Southern Baptist Convention is a large, complex, social dislocation that is difficult to interpret. It is even more difficult to predict the theology of the new Southern Baptist Convention. Still, we have had more than two decades to get a sense of the theological concerns of the new leaders of the Convention. Many of the leaders are articulate spokesmen for their theological positions, and it is now possible to provide a tentative report on what they will offer Southern Baptists, and we may even speculate how much of the vision of the new leaders will be accepted by the majority of Southern Baptists in the future.

In this chapter I will describe which parts of the majority tradition are at risk in the new Southern Baptist Convention, and in chapter 12 I will describe which parts of the minority traditions are likely to receive more emphasis in the new Convention.

Beliefs Baptists Share with All Christians

I have described the majority theological tradition of the Southern Baptists in terms of four clusters of beliefs. The first cluster includes the beliefs Baptists share with all Christians. None of these eleven beliefs is at risk in the new Southern Baptist Convention. In fact, at least two of these beliefs received reinforcement in the second article of the 2000 version of *The Baptist Faith and Message*. Concerning the Trinity, where the 1963 version had said ambiguously, "The eternal God reveals Himself to us as Father, Son, and Holy Spirit," the 2000 version says more forcefully, "The eternal triune God reveals Himself to us as Father, Son, and Holy Spirit." Concerning Jesus' full humanity, the 1963 version said that Jesus took "upon himself the demands and necessities of human nature," but the 2000 version says more clearly that Jesus took "upon Himself human nature with its demands and necessities."

That the beliefs Baptists share with all Christians are intact in the new Convention is of surpassing importance because — in my judgment — these are our most important beliefs. They are a highest common denominator. Their continued acceptance and emphasis is the greatest cause for celebration in the new Convention insofar as theology is concerned. This fact has an important implication. Though Southern Baptists are now thoroughly polarized, they continue to have good theological resources for cooperation. If we believe that these common beliefs are more important than those dividing us, then we cannot say that we are polarized about our most important beliefs. Concerning our present predicament we should add that, as C. H. Dodd pointed out in a famous letter more than half a century ago, often the most important factors in church divisions are not theological beliefs but historical factors such as experiences of distrust and conflict.[1]

Beliefs Baptists Share with Protestant Christians

The second cluster of beliefs in the Baptist majority tradition are beliefs shared with Protestants. Here the issues are more complicated. The first of these beliefs is that *the church should always be in the process of being reformed,* and it has not been affected by the controversy. No one has doubted that the church should always be in a state of reformation, and, in fact, the new leaders of the Convention believe that the changes they have made in the Convention constitute an appropriate reform of the Convention.

The second of these beliefs is that *the Bible alone is God's Word,* and this also is unaffected by the controversy. This may come as a surprise to readers who have heard that the controversy has been about the Bible. It is true that the controversy has been in large part about the Bible, but it has not been about whether the Bible alone is God's Word. What has been debated so heatedly is the technical matter of whether the original, non-extant Hebrew and Greek manuscripts of the Bible were without errors in matters of science and history as well as faith and morals. This controversial issue will be examined in Chapter 12.

The third of the beliefs shared with Protestants is the principle of *sola fide*, faith alone. This is presently the subject of a debate known as the Lordship controversy that is taking place among some conservative Protestants in the United States. The issue is whether or not a person must surrender totally to Jesus Christ as Lord in order to be saved. This controversy has not touched most Southern Baptists, and the two positions in that debate do not correspond to the two primary polarities in the Southern Baptist Convention. The belief that one is saved by God's grace through faith alone is not being publicly debated within the Convention.

The fourth belief that Baptists share with Protestants is that *all Christians are secure in their salvation*. This belief is not at risk in the new Southern Baptist Convention. However, for a brief period early in the controversy, the security of believers was debated. One of the most beloved of Southern Baptists' academic theologians was the late Dale Moody. Moody became convinced, entirely upon biblical evidence, that it is possible for a genuine Christian to commit apostasy and so to cease to be a Christian. Moody expressed this conviction in his systematic theology, *The Word of Truth*, and also in public lectures and sermons, and he was challenged by a number of different persons. Nevertheless, this issue never became widely controversial, and the belief that Christians are secure in their faith may be expected to stand in the new Southern Baptist Convention.

Thus, the first four beliefs that Baptists share with Protestants are not at risk in the new Convention. But the fifth belief, that *all believers are priests*, has been a major factor in the polarization in the Convention. The story is complicated. The New Testament does not provide a doctrine of the priesthood of believers; it provides an image, and, like all images, its meaning is indeterminate. In fact, the image has been used to refer to three quite different ideas: the responsibilities, the privileges, and the freedom of Christians as priests. The biblical teaching concerning the priesthood of all God's people emphasizes the responsibilities and privileges of that priesthood. In the sixteenth century Martin Luther emphasized the freedom of Christians as priests, and freedom is the only aspect of priesthood that is controversial among Southern Baptists today. For example, no one in the Convention has raised any questions about the responsibility of Christians as priests to pray for one another, or about the privilege of

Christians to have access to God. The controversial issue is the freedom of Christians as priests.

The former leaders of the Convention and the new leaders of the Convention have entirely different concerns about the priesthood of believers. The former leaders have understood the new leaders to be denying Christians their freedom as priests of God. The new leaders of the Convention have understood the former leaders to be asserting that, since all Christians are priests, one may believe whatever one wishes and still be a good Baptist and Christian. We shall consider these two issues one at a time.

The former leaders have felt that in their reticence concerning the priesthood of believers the new leaders have infringed upon their liberties as Christians in several ways. Here are four examples out of many that might be given. Early in the controversy a decision was made by the Home Mission Board (now the North American Mission Board) not to provide financial support for mission churches that call women as their pastors. This seemed to the former leaders to be an interference with the freedom of congregations to call pastors of their choosing.

A second example is a tendency on the part of the new leaders to devalue the priesthood of believers in favor of pastoral authority in congregational decision-making. This was clear in a famous resolution adopted by the Convention when it met in 1988. The resolution reads in part:

> Be it further RESOLVED. That the doctrine of the Priesthood of the Believer in no way contradicts the biblical understanding of the role, responsibility, and authority which is seen in the command to the local church in Hebrews 13:17. "Obey your leaders, and submit to them."[2]

Many of the former leaders feel that this call to submit to pastors amounted to a denial of the Baptist commitment to congregational decision-making through democratic processes. The Convention was meeting in San Antonio when this resolution was adopted, and after the adoption of the resolution a group of persons who were unhappy with it marched to the front of the Alamo and publicly burned copies of the resolution.

A third example is the commitment of many of the new leaders to "voluntary," state-sponsored prayer in public schools and to parental choice; parental choice is the idea that the government should provide vouchers for parents so that they can send their children to whatever school they choose, including schools in which religion is taught. The former leaders feel that these practices constitute a rejection of the traditional Baptist commitment to the separation of church and state, and therefore a violation of the freedom of Americans who do not believe in the religious beliefs and practices that the government would support by giving vouchers to parents.

A fourth example is the willingness of the Convention to provide an authorized interpretation of particular biblical texts. The important instance of this is the report that the Peace Committee of the Convention made in 1987. Referring to a phrase in Article I of *The Baptist Faith and Message*, the report says:

> We, as a Peace Committee, have found that most Southern Baptists see "truth without any mixture of error for its matter," as meaning, for example, that
> (1) They believe in direct creation of mankind and therefore they believe Adam and Eve were real persons.
> (2) They believe the named authors did indeed write the biblical books attributed to them by those books.
> (3) They believe the miracles described in Scripture did indeed occur as supernatural events in history.
> (4) They believe that the historical narratives given by biblical authors are indeed accurate and reliable as given by those authors.[3]

Two pages later we read:

> We call upon Southern Baptist institutions to recognize the great number of Southern Baptists who believe this interpretation of Article I of the Baptist Faith and Message statement of 1963, and, in the future, to build their professional staffs and faculties from those who clearly reflect such dominant convictions and beliefs held by Southern Baptists at large.[4]

These findings amount to formal, official interpretations of four groups of texts in the Bible. It is true that they are not very detailed interpretations, and it also is true that most Southern Baptists probably would agree with them, but they are nevertheless formal, official interpretations. Many of the former leaders of the Convention regard this document as an infringement of their freedom as priests to interpret the Bible for themselves.

Later I will explore the central component of these four issues, namely, freedom. Here I want to make a proposal concerning how we might handle the topic of the priesthood of believers and its relationship to freedom. I will begin by saying that it is understandable that Martin Luther, in his reaction against what he felt were oppressive practices in the Roman Catholic Church, would use the priesthood of believers to assert the freedom of all Christians to have access to God independently of Roman Catholic priests. Moreover, I believe that Luther was right about access to God. However, I do not think that Luther's appeal to the priesthood of believers contributes anything to his claim that we all have access to God. The New Testament does not associate the priesthood of believers with freedom from the tyranny of religious leaders. Moreover, the New Testament texts about Christians' access to God, such as Romans 5:1, and about the freedom of Christians, such as Galatians 5:1, do not employ the image of the priesthood of believers. My proposal, then, is that issues such as the four listed above should be dealt with without reference to the biblical image of the priesthood of believers. We should make our case for these freedoms without assuming that an appeal to the priesthood of believers adds anything to our case.

Now we will discuss the concern of the new leaders of the Convention that the image of the priesthood of believers has been used to mean that anyone is entitled to believe anything whatsoever and still have the right to be considered a good Christian and a good Baptist. This concern has been voiced repeatedly since 1979, and I found it difficult to know how to deal with it. What I decided to do was to attempt to locate examples of this claim in the writings of some of the former leaders. The most promising places that I could think of to look for this idea were books by Walter Shurden and William Tuck and an essay by Cecil Sherman. Walter Shurden made a strong case that freedom is intrinsic to the Baptist identity, but he was equally insistent that freedom must always be balanced by responsibility.[5] Tuck said that some people have seen the doctrine of the priesthood of believers as "authorizing any private interpretation, which a person may have, no matter how uninformed or isolated from the body of Christian believers that person may be," but he said that this view of the priesthood of believers is incorrect.[6] Sherman made a passionate and eloquent plea for the complete freedom of all Christians to interpret the Bible, but he nowhere suggested that this freedom entitles the interpreter to arrive at any conclusion whatsoever and still have the right to claim to be a good Christian or Baptist.[7]

My conclusion is that, while it is possible that some individual Baptists have assumed that the priesthood of believers entitles them to believe whatever they wish, no leader in the Convention seems to have asserted this. This means that the new leaders of the Convention do not need to worry about it anymore. It also means that they ought to stop accusing the former leaders of taking that position. We have enough about which we really disagree; we do not need to attribute to our opposites things that they do not believe.

What, then, is the future of the image of the priesthood of believers in the new Southern Baptist Convention? Doubtless the language — which, after all, is biblical — will continue to be used in the new Convention. The committee that revised *The Baptist Faith and Message* in 2000 initially proposed omitting the language from the preface to the revision, but, after some skirmishes, the language was reinserted into the preface. Clearly the new leaders are not as enthusiastic about the priesthood of believers as the former leaders were, so this image is unlikely to continue to exercise the influence in the Convention that it did prior to 1979.

My conclusion concerning the beliefs Baptists share with Protestants is that the first four will remain intact in the new Convention, but the image of priesthood will diminish in importance because the new leaders see it as a threat to their understanding of pastoral authority and because they suspect that it suggests one may believe whatever one wishes and be a good Baptist.

Beliefs Unique to Baptists

We have said that Baptists hold eight unique beliefs. The first three of these — believers baptism, baptism by immersion, and a believers church — have not been factors in the controversy, and we may expect them to be retained in the new Convention. Each of the other five beliefs has been a factor in the controversy.

The first of these *is the autonomy of local congregations*. In principle, all Baptist congregations are entirely self-governing; Baptists have no bishops or synods who can tell congregations what decisions to make. On the surface it seems that this belief will remain intact in the new Convention. Indeed, Article VI of *The Baptist Faith and Message* the 1963 version read simply "A New Testament church of the Lord Jesus Christ is a local body of baptized believers," and the 2000 version strengthened the commitment to the autonomy of local congregations by rephrasing as follows: "A New Testament church of the Lord Jesus Christ is an autonomous local congregation of baptized believers."[8]

But, as noted briefly in Chapter 3, there are some complicating factors. One is that the denominational agencies do, in fact, exert influence upon the decisions made by congregations through activities such as publishing literature. It is true that local congregations naturally feel some pressure, for example, to use the literature published by the denominational press, but in the end no one can force a congregation to do this, and in fact many do not. The fundamental commitment to autonomy means that, when the chips are down, the decisions concerning the life of a congregation will be made by its own members only.

The other complicating factor concerns the participation of congregations in local associations, in state conventions, and in the Southern Baptist Convention. We should first note that Baptists practice what they call a non-connectional polity which means that it is not necessary for a congregation to belong to its local association in order to belong to the state convention, or for it to belong to the state convention in order to belong to the Southern Baptist Convention. In practice, of course, almost all of the 41,000 congregations that belong to the Convention also belong to their local association and state convention.

As might be expected, associations, state conventions, and the national Convention set the boundaries of their membership; they decide which congregations may and may not be members. This selection process seems to put them in conflict with local church autonomy. Here are three examples. Some years ago the First Baptist Church of Oklahoma City was expelled from the local association because of its willingness to ordain women as deacons.[9] Second, the Prescott

Memorial Baptist Church of Memphis was expelled from its local association and from the Tennessee Baptist Convention because it called a
woman, Nancy Hastings Sehested, as pastor. Third, two churches in
North Carolina were expelled from the Southern Baptist Convention
because one of them supported a homosexual in his intention to
become a minister and the other gave its blessing to the commitment
of two homosexuals to live together. How autonomous, many people
ask, are these congregations if associations and conventions are able to
expel them in this way?

At first blush it would seem that these expulsions constitute an
abridgment of the autonomy of these local congregations. On reflection, however, it seems to me that this is not the case. Any group —
including associations and conventions — can exist only if it has
boundaries. If there are no boundaries, there is no group. It is perfectly
appropriate that a group set its own boundaries, and that is what
Baptist associations and conventions have always done. One may not
agree with the decisions of the groups to expel the congregations in
these three examples — I do not — , but it is difficult to think that the
associations and the conventions were not entitled to set their own
boundaries. It is also difficult to say that their doing so constituted an
infringement of the autonomy of the congregations. To the best of my
knowledge no committee or officers from the associations or state conventions met with the congregations and attempted to persuade them
to reverse their decisions. The groups simply decided that, as long as
the congregations embraced certain convictions or practices, they
could not belong to the respective associations or conventions. My
conclusion, therefore, is that the setting of boundaries for membership
by associations and conventions is an appropriate practice that does
not infringe upon the autonomy of local congregations.

There are two subsidiary issues here. One is whether the decisions
being made about boundaries in the new Southern Baptist Convention
are wise ones. I certainly think that some of them are unwise, but that
is not the issue; the issue is whether the setting of boundaries in and of
itself constitutes a repudiation of the Baptist heritage of local church
autonomy, and it does not.

The other subsidiary issue is whether there is a more strict policing
of boundaries in the Convention now than there was before 1979. The
answer clearly is that there is. In the past, policing was rare and informal. It was restricted almost entirely to local associations, and

associations expelled congregations rarely and with great reticence. Today more policing is being done at the local, state, and national levels, and there is no reason to think that this will change in the near future. Nevertheless, these activities in themselves do not, in my judgment, constitute an infringement of local church autonomy. For that reason I would add this fourth uniquely Baptist belief to the list of those that are likely to remain unchanged in the future.

The fifth distinctly Baptist belief is that *local congregations should seek the will of God by means of democratic processes under the Lordship of Christ*. In the resolution on the priesthood of believers adopted in 1988, the Convention quoted a biblical text that says, "Obey your leaders, and submit to them." In the final analysis, obedience to pastors is not compatible with congregational decision-making by democratic processes. Efforts may be made to tone down the stark contrast between these two forms of church government, but in the end they are not reconcilable. The unavoidable question concerns who has the final word in the church's life; either it is the pastor alone, or it is all of the members of the congregation, including the pastor, acting corporately.

The traditional Baptist belief has been that the authority to make decisions rests finally with the people, under God, of course. Article VI of the 1963 version of *The Baptist Faith and Message* says it clearly: "This church is an autonomous body, operating through democratic processes under the Lordship of Jesus Christ. In such a congregation members are equally responsible." At least some of the new leaders of the Convention do not accept this view. In 2000 they led the Convention to revise the language of the 1963 version of *The Baptist Faith and Message* to read: "Each congregation operates under the Lordship of Christ through democratic processes. In such a congregation each member is responsible and accountable to Christ as Lord." Where the 1963 version suggested that all members are responsible for making decisions for the congregation, the 2000 version disconnects the responsibility of the members from the congregation's decision-making process. In other words, it is possible to interpret the 2000 version to mean that the congregation decides democratically who its pastor will be and then loyally follows the pastor as he — and it is "he" — makes decisions for the congregation. It is not possible to interpret the 1963 version that way. The new leaders do not share the former leaders' commitment to congregational decision-making.

In fairness, let it be said again here that the New Testament nowhere prescribes a form of church government. As New Testament scholar Eduard Schweizer has said, "There is no such thing as *the* New Testament church order."[10] That is why Christians have followed several forms of church government. Moreover, it is quite appropriate that they have pointed to biblical antecedents for each of them. The new leaders who intend to assert the authority of a pastor to make the final decision for the congregation naturally call upon New Testament texts in support of their view. This is perfectly appropriate.

To the extent that the view of the new leaders of the Convention prevails, the practice of congregational decision-making will be lost in congregations. It is to be expected, of course, that in the coming years some congregations will resist their pastors' claims to have the authority to make the congregation's decisions. Doubtless this will result in unhappy and unedifying conflicts in the congregations.

The sixth uniquely Baptist belief is that *local congregations, though autonomous, should cooperate with each other.* This has been complicated in recent Baptist history because of the imprecision of the word "cooperation." How exactly does one measure the cooperation of one congregation with another? The traditional Southern Baptist way to do this is in terms of financial contributions made by the congregation to the institutions of the Convention such as the mission boards. Since 1925 that has taken the specific form of money contributed to the central funding mechanism called the Cooperative Program. In itself this clearly is not a satisfactory definition of "cooperation," because a church that is uncooperative in important ways might contribute money, and a cooperative church might have little or no money to contribute. Nevertheless, contributing to the Cooperative Program is the conventional way of measuring cooperation. In fact, the number of messengers that congregations are permitted to send to the meetings of the Convention is determined by the amount of money they contribute to the Cooperative Program.

What is happening concerning cooperation in the new Convention? Until 1979, the Convention almost always elected as its leaders pastors who had led their churches to contribute generously to Convention causes. However, now that those pastors are no longer elected as the leaders of the Convention, they tend not to lead their churches to be as cooperative as they once were. Indeed, there are now two alternative organizations to which disaffected pastors and churches may send their money, the Alliance of Baptists and the Cooperative Baptist Fellowship, and both of these receive money that once would have gone to the Convention. Conversely, before the new leaders took charge of the Convention, some — though not all — of them tended not to lead their churches to be very cooperative with the Convention. One might assume that now that they are in charge, they will lead their churches to contribute more generously.

If we consider that around 1991 it became clear to most observers that the new leaders would be in charge of the Convention for the foreseeable future, we now have a decade of experience to see how successfully the new leaders have been in leading their churches to contribute generously. While we have no information about individual churches, we do know that receipts to the Cooperative Program have grown steadily in the last decade. This has occurred at a time when several millions of dollars of money that once would have gone to the Cooperative Program have been sent instead to the Alliance of Baptists and the Cooperative Baptist Fellowship. It also has occurred at a time when central funding mechanisms in many large denominations are experiencing a decline in the support they receive from churches. The success of the new leaders in securing support for the Cooperative Program has come as a surprise to me. In fact, in the first edition of this book I tentatively suggested that gifts to the Cooperative Program would decline under the new leaders. Walter Shurden was right about this. In informal gatherings in the 1980s he had said, "When they drive the bus, they will pay for the gas." The conclusion, therefore, is that the sixth distinctively Baptist belief, that autonomous churches ought to cooperate in order to carry out ministries together, remains unchanged in the new Southern Baptists Convention.

The seventh distinctively Baptist belief is that *church and state should be separate* in order to provide maximal religious liberty in a religiously pluralistic society. It is a belief clearly spelled out in the seventeenth article of *The Baptist Faith and Message*: "Church and state should be separate…The church should not resort to the civil power to carry on its work…The state has no right to impose religious penalties of any kind…. A free church in a free state is the Christian ideal." This is an interesting series of statements. The first and last sentences contain two of the slogans of the traditional Baptist position: separation of church and state, and a free church in a free state. The two middle sentences are exactly parallel to the two religion clauses of the

First Amendment to the Constitution of the United States: "Congress shall make no law respecting an establishment of religion, or prohibiting the free exercise thereof."

Although these statements were not altered in the 2000 version of *The Baptist Faith and Message*, the new leaders of the Convention have a different understanding of the relationship between church and government than the former leaders did. Some of the new leaders of the Convention have made statements that belittle the separation of church and state — one called it the product of some infidel's mind — but neither these statements nor the 2000 version of *The Baptist Faith and Message* are the important indicators of the changes that are occurring. The important indicators are actions that have been taken by the Convention and commitments that have been made by agencies of the Convention. I will mention two.

In 1991 in Atlanta, the Convention adopted a resolution that affirmed the right of parents to educate their children according to their religious convictions. The resolution approved of "choice in education initiatives which include proper tax incentives for families," and then affirmed that it is possible for such initiatives to be fully consistent with the First Amendment prohibition against governmental establishment of religion. In plain language, the resolution said that it is appropriate for government to provide vouchers in the form of tax incentives for children's education in schools that promote religion, and it said that this is not a form of governmental support of religion. A second example concerns state-sponsored prayer in public schools. The Christian Life Commission of the Southern Baptist Convention, now known as the Ethics and Religious Liberty Commission, is committed to the principle that school teachers and guest speakers may lead children in prayer in public schools, provided participation in such prayers is voluntary. For example, the Christian Life Commission filed a friend of the court brief in *Lee v. Weissman* (S. Ct. 1992) in support of the offering of prayers at a public middle school graduation. These two actions reverse the understanding of church and state that prevailed in the Convention prior to 1979.

To this two points should be added. First, the entire notion of separation has not collapsed completely in the new Convention. One clear example of this fact was given in an article by Richard D. Land, president of the Ethics and Religious Liberty Commission, early in 2001. Land was writing in response to the proposal of the newly elected president of the United States, George W. Bush, that the government provide funding for "faith-based initiatives," that is, for church-sponsored social ministries. After conceding that it is possible to accept government money under carefully worked out arrangements, Land added: "As for me and my house, I would not touch the money with the proverbial 10-foot pole."[11] Second, in defense of the new leaders' views let it be acknowledged that it is often difficult to do justice both to the no-establishment clause and the free-exercise clause. For example, it seems to be a government-sponsored religious activity if a public school teacher is allowed to lead her students in prayer, but it seems to be an abridgment of her free exercise of religion if she is prohibited from doing so.

But even when we make allowance for these two points, it still is clear that the new leaders of the Convention will draw the line of separation between church and state differently than it has been drawn in the past. They share the traditional Baptist concern for free exercise, but they have decidedly less concern about the establishment issue than Baptists in the past. In their support for vouchers and for "voluntary," state-sponsored prayer in the public schools, they are committing the Convention to do precisely what is forbidden in *The Baptist Faith and Message* (XVII): "The church should not resort to the civil power to carry on its work." The conclusion, then, is that the nearly-400-year-old Baptist principle of separation of church and state is being revised so that in the new Convention it will not exist as we have known it. The new Convention will accept government support for religious practices, support that would have been rejected by the Convention prior to 1979.

The eighth and final distinctively Baptist belief is that *confessions that are descriptive of a people's faith are useful, but creeds that are employed prescriptively are wrong*. The Bible is the only creed of the Baptists. Two events have demonstrated that in the new Southern Baptist Convention this part of the Baptist heritage is at risk. One is the case of Dale Moody; the other is the report of the Peace Committee.

Dale Moody spent most of his adult life teaching theology at Southern Baptist Theological Seminary in Louisville. Since the founding of the seminary by James P. Boyce, all of its faculty have agreed in writing to teach in accordance with and not contrary to a brief document titled "Abstract of Principles." The document, like *The Baptist*

Faith and Message, says quite clearly that Christians cannot lose their salvation. Dale Moody dissented from that view, as we have seen, and in his classes at Southern Seminary he said that the New Testament teaches that Christians can forfeit their salvation. When asked about this, Moody explained that from the beginning of his long tenure at the seminary he had indicated to the proper seminary officials that he did not agree with the document on this one point. The question is whether the way the seminary used the Abstract of Principles is consistent with the Baptist tradition that accepts descriptive confessions but rejects prescriptive creeds. It seems to me that it is not, for the document at Southern Seminary was used not only to describe the beliefs of Boyce and the other founders of the seminary but also to prescribe what professors could and could not teach in classes in the seminary; that means that it was used in a creedal way. The five other Southern Baptist seminaries have made similar use of various documents.

How can this be handled? There seem to me to be three possible alternatives. One is to jettison the Baptist principle that creeds and creedalism are unwise. For me, and for any traditional Baptist, this is unacceptable. A second alternative is to say that the Convention generally and the trustees of the seminaries in particular have no right to place any constraints upon teachers. This seems to me to be unacceptable also. The Convention owns and funds the seminaries in order to carry out certain purposes, and it seems clear to me that the Convention is therefore entitled to place constraints upon the teachers in the schools.

The easiest way to appreciate this is to imagine a radical situation. For example, suppose it is learned that one of the teachers in a seminary is committed to the supremacy of white people over people of color; this teacher believes in white supremacy and promotes it in his classes. It seems indefensible to me to argue that, just because Baptists have no creed than the Bible, the school is not entitled to dismiss the professor. Indeed, I am sure that my readers would agree with me that the school is not only free to do so, but is responsible to do so.

So, we have eliminated two alternatives: embracing creedalism entirely or the opposite extreme, saying that trustees have no right to place any constraints upon teachers in seminaries. I know of only one possible alternative, and it is an entirely pragmatic one. It is to recognize that, while the Baptist ideal is to have descriptive confessions but not prescriptive creeds, it is not possible to live up to this ideal in the seminaries owned by the Convention. In schools, regrettably, it is necessary to place constraints on professors, and this amounts to creedalism. The unbaptistic effect of this may be mitigated in various ways. For example, we may employ phrases such as "teach in accordance with and not contrary to" the document. This does not require professors to believe everything in the document; it requires only that in their teaching they not contradict it. Again, it might help if, instead of the seminary using its own written statement, professors be asked to draw up their own confessions of faith and to present them to the seminary. Still, however much we may moderate the practice and its effects, it falls below the Baptist ideal. This is messy and unpleasant, but it is Christian realism, as Reinhold Niebuhr might say, and we can live with it and retain our commitment to having no creed but the Bible.

Also, I would tentatively suggest that what is necessary in seminaries, and perhaps also in other institutions such as mission boards in which persons are employed to carry out ministry, would not be necessary in churches, associations, or conventions. That is, a church might function quite well with members who held dissident views, even hateful ones such as racial supremacy. The church might not need to expel such members but continue to love and accept them and to admonish them to reconsider their views. Associations and conventions might adopt the same attitudes toward individual churches. Indeed, this happened in 2001 in Atlanta. The Atlanta association refused to expel two churches whose attitudes toward homosexuality differed from those of the majority of churches in the association. Most of the association did not agree with the two congregations, but they did not find it necessary to expel them. As these words are being written, a new association is being formed in Atlanta for churches who feel that it is wrong to remain in association with those two churches.

Dale Moody is the hard case because he was so passionately committed to the majority tradition of Southern Baptists and was such an energetic champion of that tradition, except on the single issue of the security of believers. The matter would be much simpler in the case of a professor with little or no appreciation for the majority tradition. It also would be simpler in the case of an issue on which a seminary's documents says nothing. That was the situation in the 1960s, when many seminary professors took a position on race relations that was at odds with the majority view in the then-segregated South. Some of them suffered for their stand for racial justice, but their situation was not complicated by their having to teach anything contrary to the documents of their schools.

The second event that alerts us to the fact that the principle of having no creed but the Bible is at risk is the report of the Peace Committee. That report, as stated earlier in this chapter, provides interpretations of four sets of Bible passages. The interpretations are limited, but they are formal and they are official. Does the existence of formal, official interpretations of the Bible constitute a contravention of the traditional Baptist principle of having no creed but the Bible? In short, yes, it does. It follows that those churches who treasure the principle most deeply ought to avoid as much as possible the practice of providing official interpretations. "As much as possible." The question is, had Southern Baptists ever offered official interpretations of Scripture before 1987? It is true that in many informal ways they have offered interpretations of Scripture. Even so innocent an act as the publication of a book or a commentary or a piece of Sunday School literature constitutes an informal interpretation of the Bible. It is not possible, so far as I can tell, to avoid informal interpretations of Scripture. Nor is it desirable. It is appropriate and necessary for a religious group to confess its faith, and, in the case of Christian groups, to offer informal and unofficial interpretations of Scripture.

But what was done in the report of the Peace Committee in 1987 was unprecedented in Baptist life. It is a very small step from that report to the Convention's saying, "Unless you accept these interpretations of these Bible passages, we will not allow you to be a Southern Baptist." And that, quite simply, is full-blown creedalism of the kind that Baptists have traditionally opposed with all their might. I conclude, therefore, that a major change in the new Convention is its apparent willingness to sacrifice the tradition of having no creed but the Bible in favor of offering formal, official interpretations of Scripture. The evidence for this is clearer in the case of the Peace Committee report than in the constraints placed upon seminary professors.

Incidentally, the adoption of formal, official interpretations is not consistent with what many of the new leaders themselves said during the controversy. From the beginning of the controversy they insisted repeatedly that the problem in the Convention was not different interpretations of the Bible but different views of the Bible, inerrancy and non-inerrancy. Here is an example from one of the original new leaders: "I do not feel that our institutions should be institutions where only one viewpoint is espoused. We should have a great breadth of interpretation of Scripture, and there is all the difference in the world between an interpretation of Scripture and an understanding of what Scripture is."[12] The Peace Committee report makes it clear that, in fact, part of the problem is different interpretations.

There are important differences not only in the interpretation of the Bible but in the principles by which the Bible is interpreted. This became evident when the Convention adopted the 2000 version of *The Baptist Faith and Message*. The final sentence in the first article — titled "The Scriptures" — of the 1963 version said, "The criterion by which the Bible is to be interpreted is Jesus Christ." That sentence was omitted from the 2000 version. The omission has become a cause célèbre and may have caused as many people to doubt the judgment of the new leaders as any single event since 1979. Numerous people have asked questions such as "What kind of Christian leaders refuse to think of Jesus as the criterion by which we are to interpret the Bible?" and "What criterion do they intend to put in place of Jesus?" The new leaders have attempted to justify the omission by saying that they don't want people to get the idea that Jesus' message is more true than the message of the rest of the Bible. The best that can be said about this is that, like Resolution 5 in 1988, this was a clumsy way to make the point.

The former leaders say we must be guided by some criterion as we attempt to interpret the message of the entire Bible, and they think that the criterion should be Jesus Christ rather than anything else. Surely they are right. The Bible is a large book with a variety of content, and it is important to have a criterion by which to attempt to interpret it. And we should remember that other criteria than Jesus Christ are available. For example, it is possible to interpret the Bible by using as one's criteria the various dispensations discussed in chapter 10. Again, it is possible to use the principle of justification by faith as one's criterion for interpreting the Bible, a position defended by the late E. J. Carnell.[13] I myself believe that the best criterion for interpreting the Bible is Jesus Christ, and I think the omission of that principle from the 2000 version constitutes an impoverishment of the confession.

Beliefs Baptists Share with Revivalist Christians

Southern Baptists share four beliefs with other Christians who have been influenced by the revivalist movement: *the need for every person to undergo a conversion, the need for all converts to be fully assured of their salvation, the priority of evangelism in the church's mission,* and *the priority of missions in the church's work.* None of these four beliefs has been an issue in the controversy, and the new Convention will continue in its commitment to each of them. Since these beliefs form the center of gravity for a great many Baptists, it is not surprising that they have been unaffected by the controversy.

Conclusion

The majority tradition of Southern Baptists comprises four clusters of beliefs and a total of twenty-seven individual beliefs. Of these, only four are likely to be drastically altered or lost in the new Convention. One is the Protestant belief in the priesthood of believers. The other three are the distinctively Baptist beliefs in congregational decision-making, the separation of church and state, and the practice of having no creed but the Bible.

Now I will offer a personal appraisal of the gravity of each of these four changes. The restricted meaning and diminished importance of the priesthood of believers is unfortunate. However, it is not a tragedy because the biblical usages of the image are still intact. Also, the case for the various freedoms does not require an appeal to the priesthood of believers.

The loss of congregational decision-making by democratic means is a tragedy. Democracy is not efficient, and it is not a foolproof way for a congregation to discern God's will — there are no foolproof ways to do that. Nevertheless, the use of democratic means for making decisions does more to underwrite the dignity of all members than any other. Moreover, it calls forth the best from all members of the church because it is they together with their pastor, not just their pastor acting alone, who are responsible for the decisions that affect the life of the congregation. Further, there is good reason to believe that a congregation of intentional believers is better able to discern God's will than any individual, including a pastor, since the congregation brings to the decision-making process a wisdom gained through the cumulative experiences of all of its members. The loss of this principle in the new Southern Baptist Convention is to be deeply regretted.

The loss of the principle of the separation of church and state is the greatest theological disaster in the history of the Southern Baptist Convention.[14] The separation of church and state has been one of the most successful components of the American experiment. The nation has held together without the glue of an official religion, and the church has flourished without the support of the government. I think that it is likely to be the case that, as government provides increased support for religious activities, more and more Americans will come to associate religion with government and therefore come to feel toward religion the kind of contempt that many of them now feel toward government. In spite of the scandals in the personal lives of some religious leaders in recent years, the American people continue to have vastly more respect for churches than they do for government. That will change as the government becomes more involved in religious practices. It has happened in Europe, where churches receive official governmental support, and it will happen here where government support will be just as real though perhaps less obvious. And the irony is that religious people such as the new Southern Baptist leaders, instead of resisting this tragic change, are welcoming it enthusiastically. They have made a disastrous mistake that will have destructive consequences for the nation, for the Convention, and for the Christian cause in America for many years to come.

The fourth fading belief in the new Convention, the principle of having no creed but the Bible, is also a tragic loss. It is very difficult to explain to people who have not experienced it how Baptists have managed to remain unified without recourse to prescriptive creeds. They have been held together by their shared experience of life in the South and their personal knowledge of and trust of each other. They also have been held together by their beliefs, just as all religious groups are, but, unlike many other groups, they stayed together without a prescriptive creed. Because they had no prescriptive creed, they have handled theological differences in an *ad hoc* manner, as they arose. It is a messy arrangement, and it is difficult to explain to outsiders how it works. But it has worked and it might have continued to work in the future. It will not be given a chance to work in the new Convention.

Does the loss of these four beliefs mean that the new Convention will be more conservative than the Convention before 1979? Quite the contrary. To be conservative is to know, to love, and to transmit your traditions. In the new Convention, four valuable beliefs will be lost from the Southern Baptist heritage, a fact that genuine conservatives must regret.

In the next chapter we will examine the six minority traditions to see which of these is likely to become a part of the new majority tradition in the Convention.

Notes

[1]C. H. Dodd, "A Letter concerning Unavowed Motives in Ecumenical Discussions" in *The Ecumenical Review* (Autumn 1949), 52-56.

[2]This quotation is from the document distributed to messengers at the Convention in 1988. The document formally affirms the priesthood of believers, but it suggests that the importance of that belief had been exaggerated by some of the former leaders.

[3] "Report of the Southern Baptist Convention Peace Committee," *SBC Bulletin* (St. Louis, 16 June 1987), 12.

[4]Ibid., 14.

[5]Walter B. Shurden, *The Baptist Identity: Four Fragile Freedoms* (Macon GA: Smyth & Helwys Publishing, Inc., 1993), 55-59. Shurden insisted on the same point in his controversial earlier book, *The Doctrine of the Priesthood of Believers* (Nashville: Convention Press, 1987).

[6]William Powell Tuck, *Our Baptist Tradition* (Macon GA: Smyth & Helwys Publishing, Inc., 1993), 64.

[7]Cecil E. Sherman, "Freedom of Individual Interpretation" in *Being Baptist Means Freedom*, Alan Neely, ed. (Charlotte: Southern Baptist Alliance, 1988), 9-24.

[8]The word "autonomous" had appeared in another, less conspicuous place in the 1963 version.

[9]In 2001 this congregation voted to sever its ties with the Southern Baptist Convention.

[10]Eduard Schweizer, *Church Order in the New Testament* (London: SCM Press Ltd, 1959), 13.

[11]Richard D. Land, "Constitutionally Safe, Religiously Dangerous?" in *Light* (Nashville: Convention 2001), 2.

[12]Paul Pressler, "An Interview with Judge Paul Pressler," *The Controversy in the Southern Baptist Convention: A Special Issue of The Theological Educator* (1985), 19.

[13]Edward John Carnell, *The Case for Orthodox Theology* (Philadelphia: The Westminster Press, 1959), 57-61.

[14]I am speaking of theology only. From the founding of the Convention in 1845 until the 1960s, the besetting sin of the Convention was identical to the besetting sin of the nation, namely, the unjust treatment of African Americans.

CHAPTER 12

THE WAY WE MAY BECOME: INNOVATIONS

Many innovations may be introduced into the new Southern Baptist Convention, including theological innovations, and some of them may be unrelated to any of the six clusters of beliefs held by minorities in the Convention before 1979. One may easily identify some of the things that have been addressed by the Convention in the past decade. For example, the Convention boycotted Disney as a protest against the sexual content of some Disney films, and it has been vocal in its opposition to homosexual practices and abortion; the justification for these actions was that these things threaten the family. They do, but so does divorce, and the Convention nowhere expressed its opposition to divorce with the same militancy. The 2000 version of *The Baptist Faith and Message* says that "a wife is to submit herself graciously to the servant leadership of her husband," and the claim was that this too was for the protection of marriage and the family. Less obvious innovations may also be under way. There may be a more negative attitude toward charismatic practices and a more positive attitude toward innovative forms of worship.

These are important issues, but I do not intend to review them here. In this concluding chapter I will restrict myself to speaking of changes related to the themes already discussed in this book. I will review the beliefs held by the six minority groups before 1979 and point out which of these are held by the new leaders of the Convention and are thus candidates for the new majority tradition.

Anabaptist Beliefs

The three Anabaptist beliefs that we discussed in Chapter 5 were the proposal that *Southern Baptists should move away from their church-type status in society and become a sect-type group;* that *they should take seri-ously Jesus' words in the Sermon on the Mount and become pacifists;* and that *they should revise their understanding of justice* away from the idea that justice is an individual's right to keep what she has made in favor of the idea that justice is the right of all persons to have decent food, clothing, housing, education, and job opportunities.

The new leaders of the Convention have not expressed publicly interest in any of these ideas. The one possible exception is that the new leaders share with Anabaptists a deep suspicion of the American culture in which they live and even of the American society of which they are a part. But the new leaders of the Convention do not express their suspicions as Anabaptists do by means of sectarian withdrawal; they rather express them by attempting to influence culture and society. So we conclude that the new Southern Baptist Convention is likely to be less hospitable to the Anabaptist tradition than the old Convention was.

Calvinistic Beliefs

In Chapter 6 we offered a revision of the TULIP acronym traditionally used to present Calvinistic beliefs to American audiences. At present the majority of Southern Baptists accept the fifth belief in the acronym, the perseverance of the saints, but not the other four — that God has unconditionally predestined some persons to be saved and others to be damned, that Christ died only for those who are the elect of God, that human beings are incapable of responding to the gospel until after they have been born again, and that God acts in an irresistible way in grace to bring the elect to salvation. What is the future of these four beliefs, which function as a cluster, in the life of Southern Baptists?

Because the new leaders of the Convention are divided among themselves about Calvinism, this question is difficult to answer. Some of the new leaders are firmly committed to Calvinism and to restoring it to the role in Southern Baptist life that it had in the era of James Boyce and John Dagg. Others of the new leaders of the Convention are just as vigorously opposed to Calvinism. Interestingly, the new leaders have not taken their disagreement concerning Calvinism into the public arena, and this has led some people to assume that they all agree about Calvinism, but they do not. This is an issue the leaders will be sorting out in the years ahead. It is impossible to tell how it will turn out.

What we can say is that, even if the new leaders decide to try to move the Convention toward Calvinism, it seems likely that it will be a long time before these ideas are known and understood, let alone accepted, by the majority of Southern Baptists. The reason for this is that many Southern Baptists feel intuitively that Calvinism undermines their commitments to missions and evangelism. The logic of this conviction is as follows. Southern Baptists hold several beliefs that underwrite their evangelism and their sending of missionaries. One is that God loves all people and wants all people to be saved. Another is that all people are entirely free to accept the gospel. And another is that if we do not tell them about the gospel they cannot be saved. Southern Baptists feel that the Calvinist belief in predestination is at odds with all of these beliefs. They ask, in a word, "If God has already predestined who will be saved and who won't, why evangelize?"

Naturally Calvinists have responses to this question. They point out that many Calvinists, including William Carey himself, have been supporters of missions, and that many Calvinists today are evangelistic. They also point out that there are other reasons for doing evangelism and missions than the ones now driving most Southern Baptists. For example, one simple reason for doing these things is that the Lord has commanded the church to do them. It is nevertheless the case that many Southern Baptists think that an acceptance of Calvinistic predestination entails a rejection of evangelism and missions, and if they think that is true, then it probably would turn out to be true. Therefore, whatever the new leaders decide, for the foreseeable future it is likely that the majority tradition in the new Southern Baptist Convention will not include rigorous Calvinism.

Landmark Beliefs

Our summary of the Landmark minority tradition includes two themes. The first is that *Baptists should separate from non-Baptists* because non-Baptists are disobedient to the New Testament. The second is that *local Baptist congregations should keep their cooperation with each other to a minimum* because the New Testament authorizes only the local congregation, and other organizations such as missions boards and publication boards are human creations with no biblical precedents. One expression of the non-cooperation of local congregations is that only members of a local congregation may participate in the Lord's Supper when the congregation observes it.

The first Landmark belief probably will not become part of the new majority tradition. Like the old leaders of the Convention, the new leaders often make common cause with non-Baptists rather than dissociating entirely from them. For example, the Ethics and Religious Liberty Commission now cooperates with non-Baptist groups to oppose abortion, and the new leaders of the Convention invite non-Baptists to address the Convention. It is true that the new leaders make common cause with a different set of non-Baptists than the former leaders did, but the Convention's new leaders are no more committed to the Landmark principal of separation from all non-Baptists than the former leaders were.

The second belief is that local congregations should restrict the size and number of denominational organizations. None of the new leaders has expressed interest in reducing the size or influence of the denominational structures. Doubtless they are as concerned as the past leaders were about the problems accompanying large, bureaucratic organizations. In fact, during the controversy they occasionally referred to bureaucratic problems as one of their concerns.[1] Also, under their leadership there was a major reorganization of the Convention's agencies during the mid-1990s, a reorganization that included the merger of some agencies and the elimination of others. But the new leaders have not expressed a Landmark-type desire to return the functions of the large agencies to local congregations. Neither have they expressed any interest in reopening the question of communion. Our conclusion is that the Landmark beliefs are no more likely to become part of the majority tradition in the new Convention than they were before 1979.

Deeper Life Beliefs

The four deeper life beliefs are that *many Christians do not know how to live life victoriously,* that *there is a secret to living a victorious life,* that *the secret is to depend upon God rather than to strive to live responsibly,* and that *those who do this will have lives that are happy and victorious.* The new leaders of the Convention seem to be divided on the deeper life beliefs just as they are on the Calvinist beliefs. Some of these new leaders hold this understanding of Christian life, and others do not.[2] On this issue, just as on Calvinism, the new leaders have not taken their disagreement public. In fact, the teachings of the deeper life have never been a matter of controversy in Southern Baptist life. During the 1990s LifeWay Christian Resources produced a series of products known as "Experiencing God," and these bear a strong resemblance to the deeper life beliefs. Still, no one has claimed that in so doing they have restored a true understanding of Christian life that had been lost in the Convention under the old leaders.

Unlike the Calvinist beliefs, it is possible for one or two of these beliefs to succeed without the entire cluster becoming part of the new majority tradition. For example, it could happen that in the years ahead more will be said about a secret of Christian living than was said in the past. The seminaries and the denominational literature could alert many Southern Baptists to the ideas that striving to live faithfully is doomed to fail and that what is needed is dependence upon God rather than striving. All of this might conceivably happen without, for example, the tendency toward perfectionism becoming as dominant in the Convention as it is in the deeper life tradition. The new leaders will have to sort out whether or not they will promote these beliefs among Southern Baptists more fully than they were promoted in the past, and it is not possible to tell whether any or all of them will become part of the majority tradition of Southern Baptists in the future.

Fundamentalist Beliefs

In chapter 9 we described three beliefs that were held in the fundamentalist movement early in the twentieth century. One is that *true Christians should militantly oppose liberalism*, which is understood as the thin edge of the wedge of secularism. The second is that *the original Hebrew and Greek manuscripts of the Bible were inerrant* not only in their teachings about Christian faith and life but also in their teachings about all other subjects including science and history. The third is that *Christ is going to return suddenly and literally to the earth and reign for a thousand years.* The new leaders of the Convention hold these three beliefs, and it is possible that these beliefs may become part of the majority tradition.

The controversy itself was an example of the new leaders putting the first principle into practice, and there is no reason to assume that they will discontinue the practice. What is not clear is how intense the militancy against liberalism will be in the future. A related question is whether ideas other than liberal ones will be opposed militantly in the new Convention. In principle it is possible that the Convention could begin militant opposition toward, for example, Calvinism or the charismatic movement. In 1992 and 1993 the Convention had noisy skirmishes with Masonry, but the militant opposition toward Masonry failed at the 1993 Convention. This is a hopeful sign, for militancy is always destructive of community and of cooperation. It is not difficult to imagine Southern Baptists who are Masons becoming alienated from the Convention if the Convention had adopted a more militant position on Masonry. If the level of militancy is reduced in the future, the cooperation and sense of community in the Convention will benefit.

Of course, the desire for community in and cooperation with the Convention was lost long ago for thousands of people who were hurt in the controversy and alienated by its outcome. Many of them have joined other Baptist denominations such as the American Baptist Churches/USA, and others have joined non-Baptist denominations. Many of those who remain Baptists no longer consider themselves Southern Baptists; some think of the Alliance of Baptists or of the Cooperative Baptist Fellowship as their denominational home, though neither of these organizations has officially declared itself to be a denomination. But it remains important for the millions of Christians still within the Convention that militancy not become a permanent feature of the life of the Convention.

The second issue concerns the Bible. From the beginning of the controversy, the new leaders have said that the issue with which they were most concerned was the truthfulness of the Bible. When asked to explain what they meant, they said, almost without exception, that the original Hebrew and Greek manuscripts of the Bible were without error of any sort in all matters including science and history as well as faith and practice.

In the new Convention there will be, of course, no retreat from this position. What is not so clear is how much effort will be made to communicate the technicalities of this view to Southern Baptist people at large. My sense is that most Southern Baptists hold to a simpler and less technical understanding of the truthfulness of Scripture. They accept the universal Christian belief that the Bible is the church's holy book; they accept the Protestant belief that the Bible has precedence over all creeds and councils of the church; they accept that the Bible is God's Word, inspired by God to help the church in its faith and life.

They have no particular interest in the original manuscripts of the Bible; their interest lies in the Bible as we now have it in English translations. They are not aware of most of the technicalities surrounding biblical inerrancy and can become puzzled by them when they learn about them. Technical inerrancy was presented in a winsome way in the annual doctrinal study book for 1992, David S. Dockery's *The Doctrine of the Bible*. It will be a long time before most Southern Baptists understand technical inerrancy, and it is not certain whether most of them will accept it or think of it as superfluous or distracting when they learn about it.

The commitment of the new leaders of the Convention to the dispensational version of premillennial eschatology is public knowledge, but there has been less said about this issue than the two issues mentioned above.[3] Certainly the new leaders of the Convention are in a position to promote this understanding of the end of the world vigorously, but so far they do not seem to be doing so.

All three of the beliefs of fundamentalism are held by the new leaders of the Convention, and all may well become in the near future a part of the majority tradition in the new Southern Baptist Convention, though it is unclear what views will be militantly opposed and whether the technicalities of biblical inerrancy will win the allegiance of most Southern Baptists.

Progressive Beliefs

In chapter 10 we reviewed four discrete progressive beliefs: *the ordination of women to serve as pastors, the critical study of the Bible, higher education as exploration rather than indoctrination*, and *ecumenism*. Those who held these beliefs were often frustrated at the unresponsiveness of the Convention prior to 1979. In a sense, their frustration may be coming to an end, not because the new Convention is going to accept their proposals, but because the new leaders of the Convention have rejected them so vigorously that it is now clear to everyone that the progressive beliefs have no future in the new Southern Baptist Convention.

The Convention rejected the ordination of women to serve as pastors in the decision of the Home Mission Board not to fund mission churches that call women as pastors. It reaffirmed that rejection in the Baptist Faith and Message of 2000, article VI of which reads: "While both men and women are gifted for service in the church, the office of pastor is limited to men as qualified by Scripture."

The Convention rejected the critical study of the Bible in the report of the Peace Committee in 1987. Its course correction for the seminaries represents a shift from the earlier commitment to theological education as exploration to theological education as indoctrination.

The fourth progressive belief, in the importance of ecumenism, is more complicated. The new leaders of the Convention have little interest in strengthening ecumenical ties with some of the groups with whom the former leaders worked. For example, through its Home Mission Board the Convention had sponsored for many years a conversation between Baptist scholars and Roman Catholic scholars; in 2001 the Convention made the decision to cancel those conversations. On the other hand, the new leaders have ecumenical commitments of their own, and they probably will lead the Convention to share in some of those commitments. The new leaders participate regularly on boards and committees with persons and groups identified as religiously and sometimes as politically conservative. The building of bridges between the new leaders of the Convention and persons such as Jerry Falwell, James Dobson, Franky Schaeffer, and Chuck Swindoll probably will continue.

The majority tradition in the new Southern Baptist Convention will not include the ordination of women to serve as pastors, the critical study of the Bible, or an emphasis on exploration rather than indoctrination in higher education. It will include building ecumenical bridges with religiously and politically conservative groups but not with mainline Protestants or Roman Catholics.

Summary

It seems likely that, in the new Southern Baptist Convention, four beliefs from the majority tradition of the past will be lost or dramatically altered. *The new majority tradition will no longer include the priesthood of all believers as it did in the past.* The new majority tradition probably will not exclude all references to this belief — indeed, some references to it appear in the 2000 version of *The Baptist Faith and Message* — , but it probably will exclude any use of the belief to speak about Christian freedom in the way Protestants have done since the time of Martin Luther.

Second, the new majority tradition will no longer include congregational decision-making under Christ's Lordship by democratic means. While there may be many years of transition and some conflict between pastors and congregations during the transition years, it seems likely that the pastor's authority to make decisions and the responsibility of members to follow their pastor loyally will eventually displace congregational decision-making in many congregations.

Third, the new majority tradition will no longer include a vigorous commitment to the separation of church and state. The phrase itself has been challenged by some of the new leaders and may fall into disuse. It is more likely that the phrase will endure but will be reinterpreted to mean principally that the government should not interfere with religious groups. The traditional belief that "the church should not resort to the civil power to carry on its work" will be displaced in more and more cases as the Convention works for "voluntary," state-sponsored prayer in public schools and for government-provided vouchers for funding religious schools.

Fourth, the new majority tradition will no longer include a resistance to prescriptive creeds. The new leaders of the Convention believe that creeds do not become pernicious simply because they are prescriptive; they become pernicious only when they are enforced in a coercive manner.

These four beliefs are all related to the concept of freedom, which confirms the fears of some of the most astute observers of the Convention that the principal casualty of the controversy in the Convention is freedom.[4]

In addition, the majority tradition of the new Convention is likely to include three new beliefs. *The first is a militant opposition to liberalism.* The new leaders have understood the controversy as a conflict with liberalism in the Convention, and it seems likely that the militancy shown in the conflict will continue in the future. It is not as clear whether there will be militant opposition to other kinds of beliefs such as Masonry or Roman Catholic beliefs, nor is it clear yet how extensive the destruction of community and cooperation in the Convention will be.

The second new belief concerns the Bible. The Convention has always held the general belief that the Bible is God's uniquely inspired, authoritative Word, and the Protestant belief that the Bible is superior to all creeds and traditions. The new majority tradition will include the technical belief that the original, no-longer-extant Hebrew and Greek manuscripts of the Bible were without error in any matters whatsoever, including science and history as well as faith and practice. While it is not clear how carefully this will be taught and how widely it will be understood, it is likely that in time allusions to "inerrancy" when speaking of the Bible may become held by the majority of Southern Baptists. The new leaders will not be tolerant of those who resist the language of inerrancy, but they will be tolerant of those who use it in the mistaken view that it refers to modern texts and translations of the Bible. Finally, in the new Convention it is likely that the dispensational, premillennial understanding of the end of the world will be promoted vigorously, and it may well become part of the new majority tradition.

Finally, the new Convention will be less hospitable to Anabaptist and progressive beliefs than the Convention was in the years leading up to 1979. This is unfortunate, as many of these beliefs seems to have exercised a good influence on the Convention. For example, even though most Southern Baptists never became pacifists, the presence of that belief within the Convention may well have served to curb aggressiveness. Again, even though most Baptists did not accept the idea that justice means that all citizens will have decent food, clothing, housing, education, and job opportunities, the presence of that idea within the Convention served to alert many Baptists to capitalism's potential for heartlessness.

The same is true of progressive beliefs. Even though most Baptists never accepted the idea that women may serve as pastors, the presence of that idea within the Convention almost certainly had the effect of assisting many young women to take seriously the fact that they have spiritual gifts and that God may call them into the service of the church. Again, even though Baptists have been divided about whether or not higher education should include exploration as well as the transmission of the tradition, the presence within the Convention of a commitment to exploration helped the Convention face up to the most serious sin in its history, namely, the injustice toward black people that was institutionalized in racial segregation and that had been a component of the life of the Convention from its beginning.

In my judgment the new ecumenism of the new leaders of the Convention is to be welcomed, but it is unfortunate that the new leaders seem to be opposed to pursuing relationships with mainline

Protestants and Roman Catholics, many of whom are fully committed to the beliefs described in the second chapter of this book.

It is possible though not yet clearly probable that two other clusters of beliefs may become part of the majority tradition in the new Convention. Calvinism may prevail, though it certainly will have an uphill battle to do so. All or parts of the deeper life understanding of Christian living may also prevail.

Many Baptists have been disturbed by the directions in which the new leaders are leading the Convention. Perhaps the most public example of this is former president Jimmy Carter. In October 2000 he wrote a letter that was widely distributed expressing his disappointment with "an increasingly rigid SBC creed." He said that he could "no longer be associated with the Southern Baptist Convention." He indicated his intention to continue to teach Sunday school and to serve in other ways his church in Plains, Georgia, and he said that he and his wife Roselynn were "trying to identify other traditional Baptists who share such beliefs as a separation of church and state, servanthood of pastors, priesthood of believers, a free religious press, and equality of women." I suspect that President Carter is representative of thousands of Baptists about whom we never hear because they lack the eloquence and the public platform needed for their views to become known.

Conclusion

Throughout this book I have offered a personal interpretation of the theology of Southern Baptists prior to the beginning of the controversy in 1979. From the beginning of the book I acknowledged happily that I respect the way we were theologically until 1979. I do not intend now to make an extended plea for readers to accept either my interpretation or my evaluation. The Convention has decided collectively to alter its course, and I accept it as a settled matter that the new leaders will continue to take the Convention in new directions. Because I still have so much in common theologically with the Convention — twenty-three beliefs of the old majority tradition, especially the universal Christian beliefs — I am still happy to continue to be a friend of the Convention. I believe that many others feel about this as I do.

Nevertheless I want to close this book with a question. It is the question that Governor Reagan made famous in his 1980 debate with President Carter. The question to Southern Baptists is: Are you better off now than you were before 1979? Many fine Southern Baptists believe that they are much better off. They believe that a course correction was needed, that a proper one has been made, and that the Convention can now proceed on the course it should have been following all along.

I do not believe this. I believe that the loss of the Protestant belief in the priesthood of all believers is unfortunate. I believe that the loss of the distinctively Baptist beliefs in congregational decision-making by democratic means under Christ's Lordship, in the rigorous separation of church and state, and in having no creed but the Bible, are the greatest theological tragedies in the century-and-a-half-long history of the Convention. I also believe that the adoption of the three new beliefs once associated with classical Protestant Fundamentalism — a militant resistance to liberalism, the inerrancy of the non-extant Hebrew and Greek manuscripts of the Bible in all matters including science and history as well as faith and practice, and the dispensational form of premillennial eschatology — does not represent any significant gain for Southern Baptists. The destructive effects of an ongoing militancy are worrisome. The call for affirmations concerning non-extant texts of the Bible has the advantage of affirming vigorously the truthfulness of God, which is to be welcomed, but its help is theoretical rather than practical, since it does not add anything to the long-standing Baptist loyalty to the texts and translations we have and by which we must attempt to live as Christians. Dispensational premillennialism is fascinating, but, so far as being able to live in hope is concerned, it does not add anything helpful to the traditional Baptist belief that "God, in His own time and in His own way, will bring the world to its appropriate end."

So, for me, this story is one of profound sadness. Others are persuaded that things are going to be much better for Southern Baptists in the future than they were in the years leading up to 1979. I pray that they are right and I am wrong. "Man proposes, but God disposes."[5]

Notes

[1]See Paige Patterson, "Stalemate," *The Theological Educator* (Special Issue, *The Controversy in the SBC*, 1985), 7-8.

[2]See, for example, the interview with Adrian Rogers in *The Theological Educator* (Spring 1988), 9.

[3]See, for example, Jerry Vines, "Eschatology, Premillennial or Amillennial?", *The Theological Educator* (Spring 1988), 134-44.

[4]In his book *The Baptist Identity: Four Fragile Freedoms* (Macon GA: Smyth & Helwys, 1993) Walter B. Shurden argues that freedom is the single most important casualty in the new Convention. See also Walter B. Shurden, "Major Issues in the SBC Controversy," in Robert U. Ferguson, Jr., ed., *Amidst Babel, Speak the Truth: Reflections on the Southern Baptist Convention Struggle* (Macon GA: Smyth & Helwys Publishing, Inc., 1993), 4.

[5]Thomas à Kempis, *The Imitation of Christ*, trans. William Griffin (San Francisco: HarperSanFrancisco, 2000), I, 19.